What Others Are Say

Clinicians who meet with gay clients wrest [illegible] know full well how difficult the zigzag path to recovery inevitably will be. Many clinicians are themselves tempted to throw up their hands in despair at the constantly recurring and seemingly insurmountable obstacles to regaining a full, intimacy-blessed life for their clients. Dr. Fawcett gives both therapists and clients a set of tools for deeper compassionate understanding and clear reasons for hopeful resolve to stay the course. His book is full of practical steps to achieve a healthy brain, a healthy sex life, and freedom from shame-based assumptions and life-limiting behaviors. Every therapist working in the LGBT community should have this rich resource close at hand.

— James Lopresti, PhD, LMHC,
Senior Clinical Supervisor, SunServe,
Ft. Lauderdale, FL

Powerful, interesting, and informative, Dr. Fawcett explores the complex and devastating effects of meth on gay male sexuality and relationships. Meth breaks down inhibition; it leaves the person open to breeching sexual templates and stepping deeper into dark areas of sexual behavior while maintaining full recall in the aftermath. He discusses how meth melds with sexuality and changes brain structure, leaving sexual dysfunction and emotional disturbance in its wake. I highly recommend this book.

— George Kallas, PsyD, PhD,
Licensed Psychologist, Sex Therapist,
The Orion Center for Psychotherapy, Inc.,
Ft. Lauderdale, FL

In this eye-opening book, Fawcett deconstructs the social, mental health, and sexual cultures of gay men and the physical characteristics of methamphetamine addiction. By looking closer at these characteristics, one gains both an understanding for the seductive nature of addiction and a basis for a rational path forward.

— Benjamin Young, MD, PhD, Chief Medical Officer,
International Association of Providers of AIDS Care
Washington, DC

Thank you, Dr. Fawcett for those who are gay men, who know gay men, who love gay men, who work with gay men...a complex topic many want to avoid, deny, dance around...you present with clarity and compassion. BRAVO!!!

— Dr. Marilyn K. Volker, EdD,
Sexologist/Gender Specialist,
Miami, FL

In an era of unprecedented acceptance and visibility of gay lives, Dr. Fawcett has focused us on the private pain of gay men caught in an addictive spiral of sexual adventuring and methamphetamine use. Dr. Fawcett is an experienced clinician and researcher who writes in a sober but compassionate way about the medical and psychological risks meth users take to escape their own internalized homophobia, social, and sexual self-consciousness. He describes in vivid detail the drug high, the instant social confidence, and heightened sexual experiences users seek. As with most quick fixes, the relief is short-lived while the medical, mental health, and psycho-social consequences compound. In particular, he demonstrates how the strong link between meth use and sex has served to fuel continuing rates of new HIV infections. This is particularly chilling as this population is more likely to have multiple partners, ignore safer sex practices, and then be marginally compliant with HIV therapies. Rehabilitation of meth users is challenging and slow, but Dr. Fawcett makes an urgent case for redoubling efforts at providing comprehensive care for this cohort of men falling into greater isolation while a life of increasing possibilities pass them by.

— Matthew Weissman, PhD,
Clinical Psychologist,
Washington, DC

Wow! As I read your book my mind was transported back to a place I had either forgotten, hoped to forget, or never remembered in the first place. The book is me. This book has an authenticity that only comes from years of working with people who have suffered at the hands of crystal meth. I needed to be reminded of the misery, pain, and sorrow that I brought upon myself as well as the hope of getting better. Any person who is struggling with a love affair with "Tina" needs to read this book! When it is released, I am going to ensure that we use this for literature readings, it is that powerful! Thank you so much for writing this and having compassion with those of us who oftentimes fail to have compassion with ourselves. This book WILL save lives.

— Aaron Michael Laxton,
Activist and Writer,
St. Louis, MO

Carlos,

I hope you find this book helpful.

All the best, David

LUST, MEN AND METH

A GAY MAN'S GUIDE TO SEX AND RECOVERY

DAVID FAWCETT, PhD

Lust, Men and Meth by David Fawcett, PhD

Published by

Healing Path Press
2312 Wilton Drive
Wilton Manors, Florida 33305

www.healingpathpress.com

DISCLAIMER

This book is not intended as a substitute for psychotherapy or counseling, nor should it be used to diagnose or treat any medical or psychological condition. The reader should regularly consult a physician or therapist in matters relating to his/her health and well-being. This book is designed to provide information, motivation, and guidance to its reader. The content of this book is the sole expression and opinion of its author. The author shall not be liable for any physical, psychological, emotional, or spiritual outcomes.

The names and personal details of any persons mentioned in this book have been altered to protect their identity.

Publisher's Cataloging-In-Publication Data
(Prepared by The Donohue Group, Inc.)

Fawcett, David, 1954-

Lust, men, and meth : a gay man's guide to sex and recovery /
David Fawcett, PhD ; foreword by Mark S. King.

pages ; cm

Issued also as an ebook.
Includes bibliographical references and index.
ISBN: 978-0-9962578-0-0

1. Methamphetamine abuse. 2. Gay men—Drug use. 3. Gay men—Sexual behavior. 4. Sex addiction. 5. Drug addicts—Rehabilitation. I. King, Mark S. II. Title.

RC568.A45 F39 2015
616.86008664 2015906872

Editor: Gail M. Kearns, www.topressandbeyond.com
Cover Design: Diane McIntosh
Interior design by John McKercher/StudioXen
Book production coordinated by To Press & Beyond

Author photo: Howard Zucker; Cover photo: Dylan Rosser

Printed in the USA

DEDICATION

I dedicate this book to Eddie Brown,
my best friend, life partner, husband and kindred spirit
whose unwavering support and enthusiasm
made this project possible.

Contents

Foreword

For more than a decade I was a crystal meth addict. They were the darkest years of my life.

I suffered numerous relapses as I struggled to get clean, and my woeful journey back to crystal meth was always the same. First, small changes crept into my behavior; not about crystal meth precisely, but other, vaguely related habits that had once accompanied my active drug use would begin entering my routine again.

A return to the gym and a shallow fixation on my body. An abandoned cigarette habit that returned in secretive fits and starts. A feeling of entitlement—to do as I pleased, to eat junk or rejoin the lurid party scene—swept over me like a declaration of freedom that hid its true intentions in the fine print.

And then the clarion call became more explicit as involuntary images of using drugs bombarded me, plaguing my sleep and my daydreams. The images became ever more seductive, promising euphoria and an escape from my own feelings.

But the most formidable thoughts that drew me back to active addiction were always about sex.

It feels ludicrous to me now. The sex life of a meth addict is as compulsive as it is pathetic. The drug ignited an obsession I had never known, taking my authentic sexuality and twisting it into something unrecognizable to me today. It was a constant pursuit of sex partners, naked video chats, pornography, and increasingly extreme and dangerous behaviors that lasted days and weeks at a time.

Even when the drug robbed me of sexual function, whenever I would visit another addict with assurances of wanton escapades that never materialized I continued to believe that the next time sex would fulfill my deluded fantasies. It was an endless loop of desire and disappointment, played out over many years.

Incredibly, I believed the allure of hot sex was worth the consequences that piled up. Visits to the emergency room. An arrest. The company of psychotic and paranoid addicts who pointed weapons at me more than once. I wasn't capable of seeing the wreckage for what it was. So, after weeks or even months away from the drug, the seduction would begin anew.

Throughout my years of addiction, and even during the recovery process, I couldn't help but wonder why. How could it be that an intelligent and otherwise healthy man would turn his life over to such a pitiful existence? What was going on in my mind? Why wasn't I able to see the lies my addiction told me for what they really were?

David Fawcett, in the remarkable book you are about to read, answers these questions and many more about the nature of addiction and the stubborn link between crystal meth and sexual compulsion. I cannot tell you how reassuring it was for me to read that there are physiological reasons for my addictive behaviors. There is comfort in knowing I am not alone in the mental changes that happen to crystal meth addicts, and that these changes are reversible.

I recognized myself on page after page of this book, including the fusing of sexuality and meth addiction, the stumbling blocks of recovery, and the deep and sometimes crippling shame that haunts active addiction and the recovery process.

Most importantly, this book maps a way back to normalcy. I am grateful to say that I recognized myself in these chapters as well, as the slow but steady process of rebuilding my brain took hold during my first years of solid recovery.

Whether you are a health care provider, the loved one of an addict, or are questioning your own addictive behaviors, this book reveals the most personal—and therefore, the most shame-filled—aspect of crystal meth addiction, and it provides guidance for a way out. Make no mistake, there is joy, engagement, and a worthwhile sex life on the other side of crystal meth addiction.

I am happy today. I am in a committed relationship that is rooted in honesty and has none of the selfishness and deceit with which I conducted myself during my dark and treacherous decade. Despite fears that my sexuality had been irreparably harmed, my sex life today is healthy and rooted in affection, love, and mutual care.

There are many avenues of recovery, but the science of addiction is always the same. This book outlines that science, while revealing the stories of addicts who, like me, have questioned if life, and sex, might ever be the same again.

Thankfully, the answer is yes.

— Mark S. King
Activist and Writer
MyFabulousDisease.com

Acknowledgments

This book is the culmination of many years of study and professional experience during which I was privileged to become intimately acquainted with the struggles and successes of hundreds of clients. Their experience and wisdom has provided an invaluable foundation for the information found here. I owe a debt of gratitude to many colleagues, especially Dr. William Granzig, whose guidance focused my studies, and the tremendous insight gained through my work with Diane Zimberoff, David Hartman, and other teachers and colleagues at the Wellness Institute in Issaquah, Washington. I am indebted to Mark S. King for his generosity and friendship, and others, including Olivia Ford, George Kallas, Aaron Michael Laxton, James Lopresti, Marilyn K. Volker, Matthew Weissman, and Benjamin Young who kindly reviewed the manuscript. I would like to thank Gail Kearns for her thoughtful editorial assistance and essential guidance throughout the production process, as well as Diane McIntosh and John McKercher for their insightful designs for the cover and interior respectively. I am very appreciative for the gifts I received from my parents and the insight and encouragement from my brother-in-law Richard Donovan. I am especially grateful for my life partner Eddie Brown, who patiently offered feedback on many drafts and provided constant support as I pursued my passions. Finally, I am indebted to my sister Susan Fawcett without whom this book would not exist. Her generosity of ideas, technical expertise, inspiration, and unconditional support made this book a reality.

Lust, Men, and Meth: An Introduction

In the summer of 2002, I received a call from a former client named Mike who, nine months earlier, had terminated his psychotherapy with me after successfully resolving a personal issue. Mike was a typical client in my private practice in Fort Lauderdale, which is largely devoted to gay men and their issues, particularly substance use and living with chronic illnesses such as HIV/AIDS.

> **It's the hottest sex I've ever had . . . I can't imagine sex without it anymore. But I've gotten to the point where I think I've opened Pandora's Box.**
>
> — METH USER

I had worked with gay men for over twenty-five years on a variety of issues, such as mental health and addictions, and in a variety of positions, including managing inpatient and outpatient hospital-based programs exclusively for the LGBT population. I felt this gave me both the experience and skill to deal with most issues confronting my clients. Nothing, however, prepared me for Mike when he walked into my office after nine months.

The last time I saw him he was an attractive thirty-eight year old man. Like many gay men, he went to the gym regularly and was careful about his health. But when he walked in that day, I was astonished to see that Mike had lost about thirty pounds and appeared alarmingly thin and unhealthy. His face was gaunt and there were dark circles under his eyes that seemed to have receded into his skull. His skin, including his face, was dry and marked with scabs. His lips were chapped and his nose was so dry that he daubed petroleum jelly into his nostrils. He couldn't sit still and nervously tapped his foot during the entire session, often squirming in the chair. He had difficulty concentrating and remained nervous throughout our time together.

Mike announced that he had a big problem, which was now out of control: he couldn't stop using drugs, most notably methamphetamine. He described the seduction of meth use that led to a kind of sex unlike anything he had ever experienced. He explained a process of rapidly violating personal limits, despite his best efforts, regarding taboo sexual activities, including casual, condomless sex with dozens of partners. He verbalized shame about his participation in what he called "perverted" sexual scenes, and he described how quickly drugs had become his overwhelming priority. He was in a near panic about his health. He revealed that he had been treated several times for both syphilis and gonorrhea, and although he still tested negative for the HIV virus, Mike lived with the constant dread of seroconverting (when an antibody becomes detectable in the blood, indicating the body's initial reaction against a viral infection). The physical toll was obvious, but that was not the end of it. He listed other costs extracted by his drug use, including losing his partner of six years as well as his job. He was on the edge of financial disaster and was about to forfeit his house.

Mike then went on to describe an even more devastating consequence of meth use. The fusion of drugs and sex had left him, as he described it, "sexually broken." He looked at the floor and said, "I feel like a sexual cripple." Mike could not imagine that sober sex could ever be as good as sex with drugs, although he admitted that toward the end of his use, the wild experiences he had when first introduced to meth were unattainable, mostly because the drug itself kept him from getting an erection. His interest in actually having sex diminished as he focused simply on getting more of the drug.

As Mike tried to get clean, he began to view his own sexual desire as an internal enemy that had to be repressed because sexual thoughts brought an overwhelming rush of cravings for meth. The only way he knew how to stay clean was to stay away from sex. I knew that Mike would have a long struggle reclaiming satisfying and intimate sex. Like many for whom sex has become fused with meth, Mike would actually need two recoveries: one for substance use and one to reclaim sexual functioning.

My experience from years of practice taught me that sexual concerns, for anyone, are a major barrier to recovery from substances, especially in the early months of abstinence. While both the relapse risk and the damage to healthy sexuality created by substance use are widely acknowledged, I discovered that there are very few solutions described in the professional or self-help literature for healing sexuality, intimacy, and the ravages of substance abuse. There are even fewer for dealing with this fusion of meth and sex in the lives of gay men.

Mike and other clients like him had a profound impact on me. I was determined to find solutions that could bring some degree of healing to these men. This search led me to pursue a doctorate in the field of sexology, and I ultimately completed my dissertation on the topic of gay men, methamphetamine, and sexual recovery.

In the course of doing my research, and later as a follow up, I posted qualitative surveys on the Internet and asked gay men to describe their experiences with drugs, particularly meth, and how the drugs impacted their sexuality, their health, and their relationships. I asked them to describe what would help them to recover their sexuality after meth, and what had, in fact, worked for them. The response was overwhelming: a total of 637 men from thirty-two countries and nearly every state in the United States responded. A nerve had been touched. I found that gay men were hungry for someone to whom they could describe their experience with meth, along with their pain and hope. They wrote lengthy, moving, and extremely personal descriptions of their experiences with sex and drugs. I was determined to understand and to help.

The nature of the drug and its ability to hijack sexual desire presents unique challenges to staying clean and developing a healthy lifestyle. Its ability to release torrents of dopamine is unmatched (dopamine is an essential neurotransmitter for the brain's reward center, regulating feelings of pleasure and well-being, which, in large quantities, creates a sense of euphoria and invincibility). The speed and strength of its addictive potential is astonishing, as is its devastating effect on the lives of those who use meth regularly. The powerful fusion of meth and sexual desire in the brain is particularly harmful, and is associated with high-risk behavior that is a significant factor in high rates of HIV seroconversion and acquisition of other sexually transmitted infections.

Mike's road to recovery was not easy. Like many, he struggled with a variety of triggers that led to multiple relapses before he was first able to put together weeks, and then months, of continuous clean time. During that early period he found it useful to avoid sex, but later was able to incorporate both sex and intimacy into his life; happily he entered into a relationship in his third year of recovery. Throughout this arduous process, traditional resources alone proved inadequate. Recovery from meth is possible, but it is a long and difficult process. There are some promising pharmaceutical approaches to relieve meth cravings, but none are currently approved for such use. Many of the men I see in a clinical setting and through web-based surveys report they were unaware of meth's devastating effects, and feel strongly that education about the drug is essential to prevent others from being seduced by it.

What I have learned about this process is contained in this book, which incorporates a broad range of tools and skills. Holistic healing practices, the need for social connection, healthy release of feelings, and an awareness of the underlying stigma and shame experienced by marginalized populations all contribute to successfully breaking the grip of this and other drugs. The notoriously high rates of relapse contribute to a sense of hopelessness for some, but many thousands of men and women have discovered that recovery is indeed possible.

After 2006, professionals across the country began noticing a decline in the number of gay men using methamphetamine. Many of us were relieved that the community seemed to understand the dramatic costs of using this drug. Most gay men knew someone who had "crashed and burned" on the drug, and its popularity waned. This pattern began to reverse after 2010, when gay men once again began showing up in therapists' offices seeking help for meth addiction. The meth on the street was of a higher potency and cheaper to buy, and Crystal Meth Anonymous meetings filled to capacity. A new generation seemed intrigued by the sexual potency of the drug, and the resulting harm began to increase once more.

The Goal of This Book

This book is meant to be a guide for gay men struggling with the issues of sex and recovery, and for the professionals who work with them. The reader will be provided not only with essential information on the problems of drugs and sexuality, but also with solutions in the form of tools and resources that will support him along his path. The book is unique in its blend of therapeutic perspectives from addiction and sex therapy, in which I have integrated the most useful concepts and tools. In addition to direct clinical care, I frequently train other clinicians who have asked for the material on substance use, identity, and sexuality in gay-identified men that is presented in this book. My hope is that these insights and tools will be helpful not only in the early stages of sobriety, but for the continuing personal evolution of recovery as well.

I have divided the book into three parts to help guide the reader through this multifaceted topic. The first part, "The Perfect Storm," examines how, through the release of dopamine and other neurotransmitters, methamphetamine has phenomenal power to change one's mood and entice the user to intake ever-increasing amounts of the drug. The role of excitement, risk, and even boredom are explored, along with the vulnerabilities of some gay men who find themselves feeling unattractive, left out, or disconnected and utilize meth to soothe these feelings. Finally, this part of the book explores the unfortunate intersection of meth, the gay community, and the rise of dangerous health concerns such as HIV/AIDS.

The second part, "Exploring the Sexual Universe," provides a sex therapist's perspective on sexual desire and how eroticism develops in the brain, an elaborate world of sexual templates, scripts, and themes that methamphetamine penetrates and distorts. This section also highlights exciting discoveries of neurobiology and the direct impact of the brain's plasticity on the profound problem of the fusion of meth and sex. Dopamine is the central player in the drama of both the feelings produced by drug use and the consequent hijacking of sexual desire. New discoveries about the brain's ability to change and adapt in response to compulsive behaviors shed light both on the harmful consequences of drug use and clues about recovery.

The final part, "Restoring Your Life," explores the process of recovery from this drug in detail, with chapters on specific skills derived from thousands of hours working with clients, managing of feelings, and rethinking perspectives on sex. The reader will find that, with increased distance from the drug, such powerful emotions as vulnerability, anxiety, or shame, which once were buried by meth use, now provide direction to promote emotional transformations that ultimately enrich both the sexual and emotional life. Finally, the reader will be guided in rebuilding relationships with himself, his loved ones, and the community as he continues in recovery.

It is my hope that many gay men and their helping professionals will find the information in these pages illuminating and motivating as they create lives of recovery from addiction as well as fulfilling and joyous sexual expression.

— David Fawcett PhD, LCSW
Fort Lauderdale, FL

▪ PART I

THE PERFECT STORM

1

Gay Men, Meth, and Sex

Brian lay on the floor of his condominium, naked and unable to force his body to move. He became acutely aware of the air conditioning vents while staring toward the ceiling. He could hear a strange whistling coming through them, and while his rational mind told him it was simply the flow of air, he was certain he also heard strains of voices and music woven into the stream of sound. He was convinced that there was a camera placed just behind the vent, silently observing everything he did; everything, including the hours of pornography that played silently on his laptop on the carpet next to him, his endless masturbation, even the nameless tricks that had been there using his meth. Brian wasn't sure who the men were, or if they were even gone, or what might have been stolen.

> **Remember when we only had black and white television and then came color TV—it's the same with methamphetamine and sex.**
>
> —METH USER

As he lay on the floor, Brian's brain seemed to be thinking faster than his body could move. He was aware of a slight tremor in his hands over which he had no control. He was aware that his nose was impossibly dry and that his side above his kidneys ached. His penis was raw from hours of masturbation. He couldn't remember the last time he had drunk any water, and he knew he hadn't eaten for days. His brain seemed supercharged and hyperalert to everything in the room.

It overwhelmed his capacity to process the mass of information his senses were collecting.

Brian was convinced that the silent camera and yet-to-be discovered microphones were conveying his every movement to the police, and he was certain they would burst through the door at any moment. He recalled another time he had been convinced the police were just outside the door. On that occasion he vacated his apartment and moved to the bathhouse for several days. Even there, he knew he had been followed and stayed in his cubicle the entire time. Now, as he lay on the floor, he tried to remember when that was, but time had become a blur.

Brian's despair after a long period of drug use is typical of many gay men for whom sex and drugs have fused together to create a downward spiral of loss and pain. The setting could be a luxurious, expensive home or the desolate street behind a bar. While the drug of choice may be alcohol, illicit or prescription drugs, or a combination of anything available, it is very often methamphetamine.

Among gay men, sex frequently plays a seductive role, hastening the downward spiral of meth-related consequences. When combined with recreational drug use, sex is a wild card that results in unanticipated outcomes. Men who use methamphetamine or cocaine to enhance sexual experiences typically discover after a period of time that they have no libido without it. Many also find, to their dismay, that using the drug impairs their sexual desire and even their ability to get an erection. When drugs, including alcohol, are used for sexual disinhibition and increased sociability, the ironic outcome is that the men who use them often eventually prefer to stay home alone with their drugs and their fantasies. It is not unusual for many gay men to find they can have sex only under the influence of substances, and that sex while sober, even after hundreds of partners over the years, is a terrifying prospect.

Of course, not all gay men are drug and sex addicts who recklessly act out in self-destructive binges. Indeed, some researchers have noted that, given the numerous oppressive forces impacting this population, it is astonishing that there is not more addiction among gay men.

It is noteworthy that so many homosexual men (and women) adapt well without succumbing to mood-altering chemicals and behaviors to escape from enormous social and personal pressures, displaying a remarkable resilience.

There is, however, a significant minority for whom addictive and compulsive behaviors have become a problem. While not the majority of gay men, they do represent a segment of our community worthy of support and understanding. The forces that influence gay substance abuse and sexual behavior affect us all, and the skills and resources that allow certain individuals to maneuver the treacherous landscape of "growing up gay" in a healthy way is worthy of study.

This book will examine one of the most dangerous—if not the absolute worst—drug to emerge in decades: methamphetamine. This man-made drug creates a burst of neurotransmitters that cause euphoria and a sense of power and virility, all quickly followed by the inevitable downsides of depressed mood, sexual dysfunction, and negative impacts on friends, family, and every aspect of life. The melding of meth's chemical properties, psychosocial characteristics of some gay men, and sex itself, presents unique challenges and opportunities to the health and well-being of our community.

Meth and Sex: A Dangerous Combination

Methamphetamine's influence on sex is infamous. Because meth quickly becomes fused with sexual desire and behavior in the brain, re-differentiating the two later on becomes a major and sometimes painful task. It is akin to separating two solids once they have chemically bonded. Most people require a considerable period of time to recover sexual desire and function without the drug, *but it is important to emphasize that sexual healing does occur.*

Not everyone employs meth for the purpose of enhancing sexual activity. The drug has a long history of use worldwide for a variety of purposes, including boosting energy to get through mundane tasks such as housework or manual labor, elevating mood when low energy and depressive symptoms pervade, and heightening concentration and even aggressiveness in stressful situations such as combat.

Gay men, however, have found that regularly mixing methamphetamine and sex is seductive, powerfully erotic, and frequently very destructive. Meth use generates a rush of dopamine, which causes overwhelming pleasurable feelings that powerfully seduce its users and instills a desire to quickly repeat the experience. Meth hijacks the brain's reward system, which is designed to make activities essential to our survival highly pleasurable. It intensifies sexual experiences to the point where the user feels that "meth-sex" is the ultimate sexual experience, and expands personal sexual boundaries, resulting in riskier sexual interaction and a heightened interest in exploring more remote corners of sexual fantasies.

Meth increases the duration of sexual activities, resulting in many users reporting marathons of thirty-six to forty-eight hours. Much of this time is spent in a drug state, watching pornography, masturbating, and voyeurism in a sexually-charged atmosphere. Some men describe the persistent erotic energy in their brains as so overwhelming that they cannot quell their sexual desire until long after the body has reached its physical limits. One man who was clean from meth noted the wonder of having an orgasm and realizing that he finally experienced relief from sexual preoccupation. Without meth, his erotic drive was able to subside in a normal and healthy way.

With consistent use, the power of the drug overtakes most users, and any pleasurable effects dissolve as meth wreaks havoc on physical, mental, and emotional health. All other needs are set aside. Even hunger is suspended by the action of the methamphetamine. Appointments are missed, bills go unpaid, dogs are not walked, partners are ignored, and HIV medications are forgotten. Many users' lives quickly deteriorate as their exclusive focus becomes obtaining and ingesting the drug and escaping into sexual thoughts and activities. Meth soon depletes the brain's dopamine reserve until the user's mood crashes to deep, sometimes suicidal depths and he is compelled to return to the drug again and again.

There are numerous ways to hit bottom with meth. For many gay men, dozens, hundreds, even thousands of casual sexual encounters ultimately result in a hollow, painful emptiness that can no longer be filled with sex, meth, or other drugs. While not everyone suffers the extreme consequences of using this drug, many gay men can describe in detail their own story or stories of their friends whose lives have been shattered by methamphetamine use. Professionals agree that this drug hits harder and faster than most others. After enough anguish, many begin a self-examination and, once in recovery, begin to accept the possibility that portions of themselves that were buried, alienated, or even despised can be acknowledged, accepted, changed, and integrated into a new appreciation of who they are.

Among the most devastating of the losses created by meth is the feeling that one's sexuality has somehow been permanently damaged. Men continue to describe themselves as "sexual cripples" during abstinence. Many are unable to function sexually without the drug. They find that nothing fires sexual desire, and many believe that nothing ever will bring it truly alive again. Even well into recovery, the ability to experience pleasure is at times elusive for those without support.

This fusion of meth and sex becomes particularly obvious when someone in recovery attempts to extricate crystal meth from their life. Sexual thoughts, sexual feelings, and seemingly casual events such as smells, sounds, and visual cues become a minefield that requires careful and conscious maneuvering. Sex, therefore, becomes threatening and dangerous because it sets off drug cues. An attractive man on the street, notification of an instant message, the sensation of walking into a bar, even getting blood drawn at the doctor's office can set off drug cravings that lead directly to sexual desires and fantasies. Many newly clean meth users even describe strong triggers evoked by walking into a Crystal Meth Anonymous meeting where one might see former tricks or simply be exposed to a sexually charged room full of gay men. This is disquieting for many in early recovery because they feel they must totally suppress sexual thoughts in order to avoid a relapse.

Such triggers heighten one's pulse, cause sweats, and induce a very real and sometimes overwhelming desire to use the drug. Even in sleep one finds little escape as the subconscious expresses its need for the euphoric rush of dopamine and heightened sexual sensations. One man from Tampa who was trying to stay clean from meth wrote about dreaming of sexual situations:

"I constantly have nightmares. In most of them I wake up right when I put the pipe to my lips or when I get the needle in my arm. Right before I push in the syringe I'll wake up in a cold sweat and be depressed that it was only a dream. I miss it very much."

For most in recovery, drug dreams are followed by profound relief upon awakening when one realizes he or she hasn't, in fact, relapsed. For the meth user quoted above, meth dreams are different. He wakes up depressed to realize that the meth rush and the meth-sex that seemed so close were only a dream.

Once the cravings begin to subside, men are often left with the belief that sex without meth could never be as intense as it was or exciting as it was with it. Many feel doomed to a life of unexciting "vanilla" sex, constantly fighting euphoric memories of sex on meth. Avoiding methamphetamine is, by itself, a hugely challenging process, and damage to one's sex life makes the recovery even more difficult and painful.

Recovery from methamphetamine is a long process of addressing a barrage of triggers to use the drug. Cravings can be successfully managed by remembering that the cue is like a wave washing over one's entire body. It has a forward motion and will, ultimately, crest and pass. At its height the urge to use seems unbearable, but by practicing cognitive techniques and applying relapse prevention tools one can survive the craving. These will be addressed in detail in later chapters.

Meth's Appeal for Gay Men

Methamphetamine is, in many ways, the perfect drug for gay men. In addition to initially heightening sexual experiences, it artificially neutralizes many concerns gay men have about themselves and their place in the community. Where there is little confidence, meth creates feelings of strength and power. Where there is fear, it creates assertiveness and even aggression. Where there is a feeling of unworthiness, it creates a sense of narcissism that is, in itself, mood-altering. Where there is a feeling of not belonging, it creates connection without concern for age, physique, or wealth. Where there is an internalized belief, based on a lifetime of messages that gay sex is wrong and shameful, it creates an exhilarating thrill at flaunting taboos and celebrating gay sexuality.

To some extent, every gay man in our society experiences internalized homophobia, a deep-seated belief that scorns homosexual characteristics and behavior not only in others, but also in ourselves. Compounding this is the difficulty of finding one's way in the sometimes harsh gay subcultures. The result is a poor self-image consisting of false beliefs, negative self-talk, or critical projection onto others. For example, a gay man might believe:

> **At 50 I don't exist socially in the gay community anymore. Having a "connection" has made me "cool"; albeit temporarily... but it's better than being invisible when I want to get laid.**
>
> METH USER

I'm not good looking enough.
I don't drive the right car.
I don't fit in.
I don't have the kind of wild sex I imagine everyone else is having.
I will never have enough money.
I don't have a big enough penis.
I need pec implants to really look good.
I no longer have sexual stamina.
I feel like damaged goods because I have HIV or some other chronic illness.
I cannot commit to my partner because gay relationships never last.

It sometimes seems the automatic voice in our heads that endlessly repeats these thoughts will never cease. This voice, which is certainly not exclusively gay, provides a running commentary, often derisive, about our thoughts, feelings, and actions. If we try something new, it may taunt us: "Who are you to think you can do that?" If we really want to go for success in love, career, or even recreation, many hear, "Don't try that; you will fail and you will be shamed." Others may hear, "If you succeed you will be punished; something bad will happen."

For many, this constant self-judgment is a virtual Times Square of brain activity with a constant barrage of evaluating, judging, and criticizing. It is obvious in critical, catty comments about others. In such cases, closer inspection usually reveals this to be a projection of one's negative beliefs about oneself. Some people compensate with material things purchased on credit that they cannot really afford. Others spend hours at the gym building their bodies to an often-elusive point when they believe they will be attractive enough. Others become arrogant and self-centered, forgetting that an inflated ego is always driven by feelings of inferiority.

At some point in their lives, almost all gay men experience deep-seated shame about their sexual attraction to other men. This may be buried under politically correct interaction or over-the-top camp, or it may be adorned in ultra butch garb. It is reinforced by men seeking partners who are "straight acting," frequently abbreviated on websites as "str8 acting." While it is natural that many gay men find masculine traits appealing, relentlessly demanding such characteristics (or even hypermasculine ones) in themselves and/or their partners reflects rigidity about gender norms and a lack of acceptance, at some level, of their same-sex attraction. Because most gay men have successfully come out of the closet, it is difficult to see these subtle remnants of internalized homophobia that lie just under the surface and exploit their perceived flaws, making them even more vulnerable to the attraction of an apparent solution such as meth.

Internalized Homophobia

When I ask my clients if they experience any sense of internalized homophobia, most will immediately deny it. After all, didn't they come out some years ago? Their families know and perhaps adore their friends or partners, their boss is aware that they date men, they attend gay pride events, and they clearly enjoy sex with other men. If one digs a little deeper, however, shadows begin to emerge regarding their feelings concerning the gay community and their own sexual orientation.

Many have stereotypic beliefs about other gay men: they are emotionally immature, they are not capable of a sustained relationship, they may be embarrassingly feminine, or they're all sex-crazed. Sometimes these broad indictments end up being a convenient rationale for excusing the speaker's own bad behavior. One client, for example, sabotaged every significant relationship when the level of intimacy reached a point he could no longer tolerate. Rather than recognize this pattern and work through his own issues, he rationalized leaving his partner by declaring that "gay men just can't sustain an intimate relationship." In other cases, a gay man may express beliefs about other gay men that only serve to separate him from a large portion of his community. Gay men are more heterogeneous than ever before, but many feel confined to identify themselves to a narrow group within the community, thus sharply limiting their experience of belonging.

Gay men have perfected the art of labeling themselves in ways that are creative, yet at times constraining to identity. After fighting to move beyond stereotypes imposed by straight culture, there is something disquieting about self-imposed categories typically based only on external characteristics and sexual behavior. This is a logical outgrowth of life online, especially sexual networking sites where gay men package themselves as commodities for quick review by the outside world. It is here that one finds clear evidence of homophobia expressed within their own community. Sometimes it's simply discrimination ("no fats," or "no redheads"), but usually there is a flavor of homophobia ("no fems," or "masculine only" or "str8 acting"). Although many men serosort (seek sexual partners who share their HIV status) as a harm-reduction method to minimize risk of new HIV infection, there remains evidence of the rift between men who are HIV-positive or negative ("disease free" or "clean"; "d/d free—UB2"). Despite attempts to buffer the impact of these qualifiers ("it's just a preference"), these terms create painful separations within the overall community.

Of course, we all have our own tastes and preferences, and we have a right to both express them and seek sexual partners who match our sexual templates. There seems to be very little consideration, however, of the impact these blunt, value-laden statements might have on someone who might happen to be overweight, or have red hair, or not be the hypermasculine male idolized by many gay men as the only acceptable version of today's gay male.

The list of gay labels is long and ever-changing, but provides people with a common lexicon by which to classify themselves and one another: bears, daddies, boys, twinks, tops, bottoms, barebackers, clubkids... even labels related to drug culture such as PNPers (someone who both parties with drugs and plays sexually) and slammers (someone who injects drugs). Some categories are broad and general, and some are more obsessively developed. They may be valuable in helping gay men forge an identity in the relatively hostile environment that we call gay life. Labels provide guidelines for many men both during the coming out process and beyond, laying out a rich menu of subcultures that provide both identity and a sense of belonging.

While labels provide a level of comfort in a homophobic world, they confine and even further divide the community as well. Members of one group may reject (overtly or covertly) others who don't belong, leading to stigma within the community. Individuals can also limit their identity to externals alone and not push themselves to completely discover who they might be as individuals, daring to express that to the world. Labels provide cover for ignoring the internal thoughts and feelings that make a person unique and, ironically for someone seeking to fit in, for what makes us both likeable and lovable as individuals. Too often gay men are complicit in oversimplifying the identity they express to the world, which only reinforces the stereotypes about their community, such as hypersexuality and superficiality. To break through the tyranny of internalized homophobia, gay men need to personalize their identities and express themselves in ways that reflect who they really are, inside and out.

Hungry to Belong

Meth boosts the self-confidence of many men who use it. There is great seduction in the power of a drug to transform someone who is lonely, tired, and feeling unattractive and invisible. Many men who have lived with HIV for decades experience these feelings, and are thus one of the more vulnerable populations for meth use. While on the drug, most users at first describe a significant increase in their self-confidence and emboldened sexuality. One man wrote, "Oh yeah, [on meth] I was able to do ALL the things I would only fantasize about and was too shy to admit to."

Methamphetamine is also very effective at numbing emotional wounds. Where there is shame or a sense of taboo, it ignites a defiant outburst overflowing with erotic energy and release. The drug takes a lifetime of feeling different and left out, and by reducing inhibitions, allows one to feel connected in a way that many gay men have never before experienced. At last they can be a member of the tribe—they finally belong. Membership is expressed sexually by a freedom to share the most intimate secret fantasies, and indeed, to act some of them out. Ironically, it creates a drug-driven sense of authenticity of, "I can finally be me and celebrate my sexuality."

Many gay men grow up feeling alienated to the point that they have difficulty assimilating into a group. As a result, they crave a sense of belonging and social grounding. Some cohesive bonds are affirming, like dancing, spiritual activities, HIV support groups, and recreational activities such as gay softball. Others, like circuit parties (large dance parties characterized by music, sex, and drug use that occur on a "circuit" made up of various cities around the world) have the potential for destructive behavior, but are viewed overall as a positive context for interaction with other gay men.

Serious users of methamphetamine find themselves sharing a similar bond. Their boundaries are reinforced both by internal group behavior and by experiencing the criticism and negative feelings within the gay community about "meth-heads." Meth users occupy a different world, sharing rituals of both drug use and sexual behavior, often using online communication for both sex and drug hookups. Even within this culture there are subgroups of users, such as slammers (injecting drug users), who share an identity. Online chat and webcam groups can be found where visual images of slamming are depicted or even shared in real time. Methamphetamine then, as a gay cultural phenomenon, can serve to define a group of men who feel a sense of belonging, just as tribal tattoos, certain clothing, and jewelry make a statement about identity.

When the consequences of meth eventually make continued use of the drug impossible, as happens to many, those feelings of unworthiness, shame, and being marginalized come crashing down on the user. They are compounded by depression, sometimes extreme, that accompanies withdrawal from the drug. Meth users are left not only with significant wreckage in their lives, but also with a desperate hopelessness. In many cases, they have new concerns to address, such as a lost relationship, unemployment, legal problems, or new health issues such as HIV or hepatitis.

The cruel paradox with methamphetamine and other drugs is that these feelings of confidence and belonging are all an illusion. Meth ultimately increases isolation and loneliness, and eventually creates even more stigma for a tribe of gay men by dividing the community itself. It adds another layer of shame in the form of a cruel drug that makes men lie to their friends, cheat on their lovers, and ignore their responsibilities. Ultimately it fuels and reinforces their innermost fears that they are, indeed, flawed.

Are Gay Men at Higher Risk?

Numerous studies have tried to determine differences in the rates of addiction for homosexuals versus heterosexuals, and to ascertain if they are changing over time. While there are no conclusive numbers, it has been noted that rates of substance abuse among gay men seemed to drop from studies in the 1970s, when rates of alcoholism for gay men were said to be as high as 30 percent.[1] These high numbers are partially explained by the research methodology for these early studies that relied heavily on an oversampling of bar patrons.

With the AIDS epidemic, research methods captured a better representation of gay men, resulting in studies in the 1980s that revealed lower rates of addiction. One study, for example, found the rate of heavy drinking for gay men in San Francisco to be 19 percent, compared with 11 percent among heterosexual men in the sample.[2] This study also found that gay men used a greater variety of drugs than their heterosexual neighbors, but actual differences in the frequency of drug use were relatively minor.

More recently, studies have shown that gay youth and young adults continue to have high rates of substance use, particularly alcohol. There is much discussion about the use among gay men of drugs such as methamphetamine, ketamine ("K"), gamma hydroxybutyrate ("G"), and even poppers, yet alcohol continues to be the most widespread, destructive substance of abuse. This is not unexpected, given the role of gay bars as a central focus of the community, the prominence of alcohol advertising targeting the gay community, and social norms regarding substance abuse. While the actual prevalence of gay substance abuse varies from study to study, and from drug to drug, it is clear that being homosexual is a significant risk factor for addiction.

Early initiation to substance use is not the only difference between homosexual and heterosexual youth. Lesbian, gay, and bisexual youth show patterns of drinking over time that increases more rapidly than substance use by heterosexual youth.[3] In one study of young gay men (termed YMSM, or "young men who have sex with men"), 84 percent had used alcohol in the last thirty days, and 21 percent qualified as binge drinkers.[4] Even given the prevalence of drinking and binge drinking among youth of similar age and of any sexual orientation, this rate is high.

In addition to early onset of drinking and drugging, other experiences of gay youth have a significant impact on their health as adult men. One study, for example, found that forced sex, gay-related harassment, and physical abuse were associated with negative health outcomes for adults, including higher rates of HIV infection, partner abuse, and depression.[5]

Finally, there are differences among groups of gay men who use drugs. One study found that HIV-positive gay and bisexual men who also inject drugs are a distinct group from other HIV-positive gay and bisexual men.[6] More of the injection drug users reported sex with women and identified themselves as "barebackers" (having sex without a condom). Their sexual risk behaviors were similar to other men who used drugs (but not injection), although both groups had more condomless sex than gay men who didn't use drugs at all. The gay injection drug users also reported more use of non-injected methamphetamine, amphetamine, barbiturates, and gamma hydroxybutyrate (GHB) than non-injection gay drug users, as well as more sexual abuse, anxiety, and hostility.

Let's Talk About Meth

The subject of meth in our society, the media, and even among addictions professionals sparks a lively discussion. Many professionals insist that methamphetamine is simply the "drug du jour," the current drug that will grow in popularity, peak, and then slowly fade out in popularity as another drug takes its place. They describe media attention to methamphetamine as hysterical, purposely created to manufacture an unrealistic fear of the drug. Some professionals argue that addiction is not inevitable from the "first toke," and that many users are able to enjoy methamphetamine casually.

> **Gay men need to have lives they desire, respect, and are proud of if they are going to kick this thing.**
>
> — METH USER

My experience with meth comes from years as a psychotherapist and drug counselor. The people who come into my office have suffered major consequences from the drug and want to stop using. They wouldn't be in my office if they didn't have a strong desire and motivation, through losses of health, jobs, partners, homes, and friends, to purge this drug from their lives. It can be reasonably argued that people who are able to use the drug on occasional weekends for energy and as an augmentation for sex do not need to seek out assistance with therapy. There are plenty of gay men, however, for whom meth use has spiraled out of control and who cannot extract themselves from its grip.

It is important to approach the whole intersection of methamphetamine and gay men both with respect and an awareness of our own judgments and opinions. Hysterical and dire warnings about the devastating consequences of the drug and the demonization of those who use it accomplish little except to compound the shame and stigma already felt by the drug abuser. Like many others, early meth awareness campaigns featured scary images of the impact of this drug. One such campaign showed an image of a meth user whose skull was exposed, and many of the physiological consequences, including dental and skin problems, were highlighted. Much of what this frightening image showed was indeed true, and perhaps a few men gained some information about the consequences of using the drug.

However, the skull image had the greatest impact on those who did not or would not use meth in the first place. They were especially horrified, and many expressed negative opinions about anyone who would use this drug, creating a divide within the gay community. Ironically, upon witnessing these campaigns many of those who did use the drug withdrew even more into their meth lives and their meth contacts, digging themselves into a life kept secret from their non-using friends.

Anyone hoping to have a positive impact on this epidemic must employ both respect and empathy, and not further stigmatize the men and women caught in this drug vortex. Hearing that I was conducting surveys on gay men and sex, one man said, "I hope you don't use the information you collect against the community to make us look like a pack of strung out perverts. You can't put that on all of us."

People under the influence of methamphetamine and other drugs exhibit behaviors that they would not ordinarily display—sexually, socially, and emotionally. The drug takes a terrible toll not only on friends and family, but mostly, of course, on the user. Individuals must take responsibility for their behavior, but they need support in this effort. One client wrote, "I know I'm preaching to the choir, but it's so important to remember that each drug user is a person. Many of them are otherwise intelligent. They should always be treated with respect, especially when they don't have it for themselves. It does make a difference."

Substance abuse treatment approaches that use confrontation to break through resistance and denial are not well suited for this drug. While healthcare professionals are sometimes shocked when listening to accounts of meth-fueled sexual acts or fantasies, it is critical not to further shame the user. Most are fully aware of their behavior and are shocked by it themselves. Many are frequently traumatized by the dark thoughts and fantasies that bubbled up from their own subconscious while on the drug. This further drives someone in recovery into a defensive mode that makes getting in touch with feelings and emotional growth even more difficult.

Family and friends are often badly hurt by someone's drug use and find it difficult to provide support. If this is the case, the user should be directed to obtain support elsewhere, from a self-help group or therapy. In those supportive contexts the user can be encouraged and empowered to begin making the necessary changes in his life, empowered by collaboration with others making the same journey. Affected friends and family may also find healing through support groups or therapy.

The negative feelings weighing down a recovering person, especially in sexual areas, must be lifted. Building lives for which they have respect and pride begins with ridding themselves of taught shame and learning self-acceptance and self-affirmation.

As a community, gay men must acknowledge the impact of meth (and other drugs) and begin to talk about it openly. Our community is divided about methamphetamine, along with other drug use, and its effects. Many have outspoken judgments about the drug, which ends up driving the issue further underground. Others cannot relate to the issue at all and consequently feel little urge to take action. In an online survey of meth users, one man described this estrangement:

> *Here in Southern California we seem to have three sets of folks with regard to methamphetamine: 1) the folks who will or are currently using, 2) the folks who have quit and are so busy preaching about how wonderful they're becoming that they forget (or don't know) how much more difficult this attitude makes it for others to quit, and 3) the folks who've never used and sit back in judgment of those who do, while, of course, they sip their Bloody Marys and Screwdrivers.*

Dialogue is needed to begin to address methamphetamine and drug abuse in the gay community in general, and to create a culture of safety for those who are desperately trying to heal their lives, including their sexual lives. We have an enormous elephant in the room that many are struggling not to recognize. Having placed the use of methamphetamine in the context of the larger gay community, it's necessary to examine exactly how this potent drug, once ingested, has such a powerful physical and emotional impact. That is the point at which meth hijacks the pursuit of pleasure.

2

The Hijacking of Sexual Desire

A bright beam of light shines out of the dark, illuminating a sea of beautiful, dancing, shirtless men. They are young and sexy, with muscular, shaved bodies and ecstatic expressions on their faces. They move to the rhythm of a DJ's energetic mixes. Above their heads, in the dark, the room is filled with hundreds of bright, shining crystals, giving the entire scene an eerie, out-of-this-world appearance.

Indeed, it isn't this world. This is an advertisement printed in glossy color appearing in a local gay magazine, typical of many across the country. The shimmering lights have been created by an airbrush, and the text has been carefully worded to include the phrase "crystal nights."

> **I truly believe meth has damaged my ability to enjoy normal sex.**
>
> — METH USER

The ad is coded, and not very subtly, to convey the presence of methamphetamine at this dance party. Another ad in this paper includes an appearance by "Tina" (a common name for crystal meth) and other drag queens promising an evening of entertainment. The ads aim to connect meth, in the reader's mind, with sexiness, fun, energy, belonging, and a seductive altered state. They also subtly normalize meth in gay life, helping many men make the assumption, "everyone is doing it, why shouldn't I?"

This kind of marketing is one of the ways that methamphetamine is introduced and reinforced in the lives of gay men. There are many other routes. Some men are introduced to meth by a sex partner or friend whose description of its sex-enhancing properties makes it seem nearly irresistible. Others impulsively decide to try meth in the heat of the moment, accepting a stranger's offer in the darkness of a bathhouse cubicle or while dancing at a circuit party.

With ongoing use, many quickly find themselves falling into a crystal vortex, pulled in by the powerful energy of meth fused with sex, unable to extricate themselves and to stop using. Some of these men slip into a rapid decline, their existence dominated by meth. At first they believe they can maintain control over their use of the drug, firmly vowing that their ability to plunge into the seductive swirl of drug-enhanced eroticism won't stop them from pulling back to the safety of their daily lives. Indeed, some do manage their use, but many lose nearly everything. Some will lose their lives.

How is it possible that this drug holds such power over so many people, gay and straight alike? Other drugs have been associated with enhanced sexual activity in the past. Cocaine, for example, could distort sexual desire, resulting in sexual dysfunction. Once in recovery from cocaine, however, most were able to rebuild their sex lives relatively quickly. Meth, on the other hand, appears to have longer-lasting effects and a tighter hold on sexual associations. Indeed, meth uniquely ravishes a user's brain and body. The differential impact of these two drugs lies in the brain's reward center.

When meth, like other amphetamines, is introduced into the body, it acts primarily on the reward center of the brain, stimulating a rush of dopamine and other neurotransmitters that create pleasurable feelings. The reward center is an area of the brain that is hard-wired to make activities that are necessary for survival, such as eating and sex, gratifying. Cocaine stimulates the reward center as well, but it is meth's duration of action—lasting up to twelve hours—that makes the drug popular for prolonged sexual experiences. And, it is this long action that brings particularly toxic consequences.

Unlike cocaine, which is a naturally occurring molecule from the coca plant, methamphetamine is a man-made molecule that is larger and ultimately not absorbed by the body. Because of its size, the methamphetamine molecule sits on the neurotransmitter receptors for a longer period of time, thereby increasing its toxic effects. Even worse, and unlike cocaine, methamphetamine not only blocks the receptors, but ultimately destroys the neurons themselves, creating a functional brain injury. This explains the long process required for recovery of cognitive skills, especially verbal, after the user is abstinent from meth. The brain must literally "rewire" by creating new neural pathways, a process that takes up to twenty-four months. This is visually portrayed with stunning impact on scan images of the brains of recovering meth addicts made with functional magnetic resonance imaging (fMRIs) which measures blood flow in the brain. Normal dopamine levels, indicated by bright reds and oranges, only begin to reappear after a year or more of abstinence.

Methamphetamine's power to release dopamine—the pleasure transmitter—is striking when compared to other pleasurable activities and drugs that also release this neurotransmitter. Studies reveal the startling contrasts.[1,2] Food consumption stimulates a release of about 150 units of dopamine, whereas sex without methamphetamine creates a release of about 200 units of dopamine. Nicotine, well known for its highly addictive properties, produces 250 units, even higher than food and sex. Cocaine, known to trap many users into a powerful craving for the drug, releases about 350 units of dopamine. Methamphetamine, an artificial substance that overwhelms the brain's ability to process it, releases a torrent of nearly 1100 units of dopamine, nearly three times that of cocaine.

These findings and my clinical experiences with hundreds of men caught in the vortex—and harmed in ways they don't understand—convince me that methamphetamine is not just another "drug du jour," but a toxic substance that hijacks the brain at previously incomprehensible levels, snaring many of its users into a painful addiction from which escape is extremely difficult.

The Fusion of Meth and Sex

The sex-enhancing properties of crystal meth quickly cause the brain to link the drug with an intense, cerebral sex trip. This pairing is repeatedly amplified by the power of the sexual drive, and soon the effects of meth become indistinguishable from sexual feelings. Methamphetamine, even more than cocaine, fuses with the user's inner sexual life and its most secret desires and fantasies. It supercharges sexual drive and self-confidence while powerfully rewarding the pleasure of sex.

The strong bond between meth and sex is not just a gay phenomenon. Some scientists theorize that women find methamphetamine more desirable than cocaine as a sexual drug because its longer duration allows the slower buildup of sexual energy conducive to female sexual pleasure. In a study of northern California heterosexuals, it was reported that many experienced increased desire, increased number of partners, and unsafe sex practices after using meth.[3]

Nor is meth use limited to its sexual effects. Some women and a small percentage of men report using meth for energy to fuel long hours at the office, complete mundane tasks, reduce appetite, or keep up with dawn-to-dusk homemaking activities. They report no erotic association, and in fact are sometimes puzzled at the drug's sexual properties. Still, enhancement of sex seems to be the most common reason for meth use.

In a web-based survey I completed in 2004, over one hundred men rated why they used meth and the relative appeal of that effect. I inquired about antidepressant effects, relief of boredom, increased personal sexual attractiveness, increased energy, and increased sexual desire. Respondents scored their answers based on a Likert scale of five choices: "very little," "little," "moderately," "much," and, "very much."

All five of meth's effects held allure for men using the drug, but some were more sought after than others. Meth is a powerful antidepressant, at least temporarily, because of the flood of dopamine it promotes. Any antidepressant effects, however, are quickly negated by the inevitable crash of mood caused by the depletion of dopamine that follows intensive periods of meth use. Thirty-four percent of men in this survey reported using meth "very much" to relieve symptoms of depression. A slightly higher percentage of men, thirty-seven percent, stated that they used meth to relieve boredom. Ingesting the drug to increase energy as well as increase personal sexual attractiveness were very closely ranked at forty-six percent and forty-seven percent respectively. The most desirable effect rated by men in this survey was enhancing sex, a quality rated by sixty-four percent of the men as something they desired "very much."

It is important to remember that a pleasurable sex life after meth can be reclaimed, but the bond between meth and sexual desire must be broken. This is addressed in greater detail in later sections on the brain and the recovery process. In helping clients break this bond, I find that information is power. Having a clearer understanding of the problem of, "what is meth and what is me," becomes a powerful tool for recovery. In this spirit, it helps to understand how the drug interacts with several critical aspects of sexuality: desire, behavior, and performance.

Lust, Love, and Desire

For many users, meth makes sexual desire go nuclear. Men describe their sexual lust ramping up to the point of powerful obsession. Even after hours of sexual activity, including orgasm and persistent masturbation, sexual desire continues to burn.

Of methamphetamine's consequences on various stages of the sexual cycle, the most profound is on sexual desire, which consists of sexual fantasies and the subsequent drive for sex that they ignite. Sexual desire results from complicated interactions between our *relationship with ourselves* (that is, our core beliefs about self-worth, self-acceptance, brain chemistry, and history with persons significant in our lives) and a range of other emotions and situations that fuel or dampen our arousal.

Increased sexual desire is expressed in many forms, but most men who take meth report a preoccupation with sex. One man expressed a typical experience when he wrote: "I turn into a little whore when I'm on meth, and, as a result, I crave sex all the time." Feeling sexually desirable is a problem for many gay men as they age, especially for those living with HIV. Men who have been HIV-positive for fifteen or twenty years are particularly vulnerable. They often have less energy, lower libido, are more isolated, and have reduced self-esteem; meth appears to be the perfect solution to re-energize their lives.

Sexual desire requires some deconstruction in order to understand how it is affected by meth. Two key components of desire are lust and love. Lust is described by Jack Morin as "providing the zest that makes sex fun and self-affirming." Lust separates the physical from the emotional, transforming the sex partner into an object to be used for one's own benefit. Lust fuels both arousal and orgasm.

Love, on the other hand, idealizes ones' partner. Love develops from our emotional attachments with caregivers and later with other individuals who are close to us. The loving component of an intimate relationship is a powerful bond that allows us to empathize with our partner and develop intuition about their needs and feelings that in turn allows the development of an intimate closeness. In the early, intoxicating stage of a romantic relationship, called limerence, the loving feelings of preoccupation with our partner are nearly overwhelming.[4] Limerence fades as a relationship progresses into new phases, but the level of intimacy can remain high as a couple continues to grow in their relationship with themselves and each other.

Lust and love do not always coexist in balance. They can be merged together or totally separated.[5] Most sex therapists feel that at least some degree of balance and overlap is appropriate for a healthy and satisfying relationship. Where love and lust are fused together, sex must always be accompanied by love. This occurs when someone's discomfort with sex is neutralized by "falling in love," even when such feelings may be inappropriate. This subconscious strategy to negate uncomfortable lustful feelings by interpreting them as love is more often seen in women than men. Casual sexual experiences are overlaid with a framework of "love." Unfortunately, many who infuse lust with love are frequently disappointed when they realize that their loving feelings are not reciprocated.

Men more often have the reverse situation: a complete separation in which the purity of tender love must be separated from animalistic lust. Even without methamphetamine, when lust is detached from emotion, erotic attention narrows with what Morin calls, "laser-like focus for maximum genital arousal,"[6] resulting in a particularly intense sexual experience. It is this process that methamphetamine further amplifies, virtually excluding affection and tenderness from sex. A major goal for sexual recovery is to develop a level of comfort with both love and lust where there is at least some degree of overlap.

When meth is combined with sex, one of the primary effects is a chemically based increase in lustful feelings, with resulting objectification and a decrease in empathy. Sexual partners lose their "human" qualities and slowly merge into the landscape of the meth user's fantasy. When one is under the influence of lust, partners are objectified for their physique or other characteristics. Focus turns to biceps, age, penis size, or even a glowering facial expression conveying judgment or anger. While in this drug-intensified "hunt" mode, other men are viewed simply for their sexual qualities. While some objectification is a normal component of sexual desire in any man or woman, with meth it is supercharged.

As objectification of another person increases with meth use, the ability to empathize with them decreases. Empathy is the ability to identify with another person's feelings and is a critical component of any mutually satisfying sexual interaction. Empathy enables a deeper and more intimate sexual connection to unfold through both giving and receiving, pleasuring and being pleasured. This balance is disrupted by meth, which seems to turn off those parts of our brain essential to emotionally connecting with another person.

I have discovered through my clients that methamphetamine's distortion of an empathic connection is paradoxical, because what seems real and vivid often turns out to be the opposite. For some, the drug promotes the sensation of a super-intense interpersonal connection. Many users describe this as deeper and more powerful than any they have ever experienced. The irony is that these "connections" ultimately disintegrate and leave the user feeling lonely, disappointed, and exploited. Many ultimately prefer to drift into their sexual fantasies and masturbate rather than engage with other men in "real time." Respondents to my online survey powerfully described this phenomenon. "Crystal sexually stimulated my brain so much that it replaced actual companionship. Porn and masturbation or watching other guys were the activities I got trapped into." Another man experienced a similar pattern: "I recognize that the idea of sexual contact on meth is often more stimulating than the actual sex. It's almost as if I'd rather masturbate than mess with a sexual partner."

There are some individuals who appear to be able to use methamphetamine and other drugs during sex without paying the heavy price experienced by most. For example, on the topic of meth and sex, one survey respondent wrote, "many call it 'plastic sex' with no real meaning...but I have to disagree in part. When it all clicks with the right person, it has been amazing and often almost spiritual."

Most men I have seen in my office would prefer to have full control over their use of methamphetamine, but few can truly maintain it. The seduction of fantasy is great and after a point the return to reality, frequently accompanied by loneliness and consequences of addiction itself, is a painful experience. The price ultimately paid by most meth users is a gradual separation from self-awareness and their ability to relate to other people on an emotional level. One man, returning from a third relapse, said, "I've lost me...I feel like a ghost of myself."

The primary attraction of meth for most users, as described above, is increased sexual desire, but it has consequences on other aspects of sex as well. The experience of thousands of men and women both anecdotal and in academic literature sheds light on meth's negative impact on both sexual behaviors and sexual performance, which are described in the following sections.

Meth's Impact on Sexual Behavior

1. Reduced Inhibitions and Impulse Control

Methamphetamine reduces inhibitions for almost all its users. Psychological controls that limit sexual behaviors are weakened under the influence of the drug. Powerful emotions such as shame, guilt, and anxiety that normally dampen erotic thoughts are minimized while sexual lust is ignited. A man who is typically inhibited about pursuing sexual liaisons will become fearless on meth, throwing self-consciousness aside and feeling transformed into a different person.

Meth disinhibits one's erotic imagination as well. It allows long-repressed sexual thoughts, feelings, and fantasies to overflow into real behavior, sometimes to the shock of the user himself. Many men report that sex on meth frequently results in sexual behavior they would never ordinarily consider. One man wrote: "It has made me crave sex, and I have more sex with more people, more often." Another man noted that sex becomes more wild than mild. "For me it makes sex much more uninhibited—I'm a total pig on the substance."

Breaking taboos releases an erotic energy expressed by reveling in outrageous behavior, a new experience for some gay men long bound by individual and social restraints. Profiles on gay sex networking sites often emphasize not only barebacking, but also other "pig" behaviors involving, by mutual consent, rimming, water sports, fisting, multiple partners, or other unsafe scenarios that can be demeaning and abusive. The sexual frenzy described by many men on meth appears to separate this drug-induced behavior from other traditional bondage and discipline or sadomasochistic (BDSM) activities in which a clear, drug-free head is considered vital for mutual safety.

Some professionals believe that the drug itself does not cause the excessive and risky sexual behavior, but that certain gay men are drawn to the drug because it allows them to behave in ways that they have always desired but were unable to express. While this may be true for some, many others engage in sexual behavior that they never even fantasized about before using meth, leaving them stunned at their loss of control. Whether meth allows one to fulfill secret desires or whether it fuels the creation of new fantasies, the endpoint for problematic users is accompanied by sexual dysfunction and tremendous remorse and shame.

Impulse control is a phenomenon directly related to this disinhibiting process. Meth results in much more impulsive behavior, including high-risk sexual activities such as condomless anal intercourse. Poor judgment and serious consequences often result when the brain's ability to resist urges is so dramatically diminished. One client succinctly stated, "There could be a bowl of condoms on the bed next to me and I wouldn't consider interrupting my sexual lust to use one."

Promising research will better inform our future understanding of other factors that contribute to high-risk sexual behavior among some gay men. One study,[7] for example, reported that gay men may be particularly vulnerable to impulse control disorders, including sexual acting out, gambling, risk taking, and even shopping and credit card abuse. Methamphetamine amplifies these impulsive tendencies while reducing or totally negating any innate ability to resist the impulse and avoid destructive behavior.

2. Indiscriminate Sex Partners

Meth also affects choice of sex partners as many men quickly lower their standards or personal criteria for sex partners that they might have had prior to ingesting the drug. One man wrote, for example, "I lost healthy inhibitions and learned to take too many risks. I allowed too many complete strangers to fuck me silly. Some were violent, weird, and dangerous."

Concern about the HIV status of a partner is also frequently overlooked. Gay men combining meth and sex often avoid discussion of HIV status with a "don't go there" attitude. Many attribute this to a numbing caused by years of safe sex messages, as well as the ongoing stigma of being HIV-positive within the gay community. Many men who use meth are already HIV-positive and report resentment at feeling like "damaged goods." Avoiding discussion of serostatus is both an act of resistance and denial. For many, the immediate sexual moment is all that matters. This man, for example, stated, "I don't care whether the guy is poz or neg or even has anything else." As a result, rates of HIV as well as other sexually transmitted diseases remain at high levels in cities with a high population of gay men, such as Fort Lauderdale, New York, and San Francisco.

In addition to a willingness to have sex with just about anyone, the number of sexual partners also rapidly escalates. One man wrote that he went from three partners in a year to three partners a day while on crystal meth. Such promiscuity is well documented in many studies, indicating that men using crystal have reported hundreds if not thousands of lifetime sex partners.[8,9] This behavior quickly becomes indistinguishable from sex addiction, in which there is a clear cycle of preoccupation with sex, ritualization of the process of getting sex, acting out sexually, and finally shame and despair.[10] Compulsive sex becomes a means by which to cover emotional pain. Countless sex partners, whether through compulsive sex, sex addiction, or meth-sex, results in unsatisfying and hopeless attempts to recapture that "great" sex that only exists in a memory.

3. Exotic and Rough Sex

Many gay men have found that using methamphetamine allows dark sexual fantasies that they find both shocking and traumatic to emerge. They become highly concerned that such aggressive, rough, and even sadistic scenarios could spring from their own imaginations. Meth frequently results in a significant increase in kinkier sex, and most men report pushing their personal sex play limits with activities such as fisting or BDSM. One man wrote: "When I was using [meth it] definitely made it easier to play the extremes. I share at meetings that I used to walk into a hotel room with ten guys I never met, throw them the rope, and say, 'take me however you want me, boys.' I was once fucked without condoms by over twenty guys in one night in a rather long S/M session."

Almost every respondent to my survey cited increased interest in "non-vanilla" sex. This man, for example, reported that meth, "brought me into lower and lower acts of depravity, causing me to become disgusted with myself. I would then use sex to punish my feelings." Many times individuals are left with shock at their behavior, as well as a large dose of shame that must be addressed clinically to promote recovery.

4. Aggression

Aggression contributes to heightened desire, and meth fuels aggression through its impact on serotonin, another neurotransmitter. Serotonin contributes to the quality of our sleep, mood, behavior (including violence), and impulsiveness. One man wrote: "[Meth] made me much more aggressive and a bit careless when it came to playing safely. I never quite veered off as far as others have, but it's pushed both my personal boundaries and preferences of rough and more adventurous sex out of the boundaries they once held." The increase in aggression is directly related to the increased narcissism of a meth user and the consequent decrease in empathy described above.

Worldwide methamphetamine use has been associated with increased levels of violence in both its manufacture and distribution. While few gay men manufacture meth themselves, they form a critical market segment for the drug; some become involved in local distribution, which is fraught with legal risk and danger. Meth notoriously causes paranoia and aggression, resulting in physical abuse of both partners and family. Among gay men, the level of hostility incorporated into sexual "play" is, in my opinion, amplified by the drug, resulting in aggression directed outward at others through rough sex and inward through self-hatred, allowing oneself to be demeaned, for instance, with rough anal sex or as the recipient of multiple ejaculations by numerous men.

Aggressive tendencies in meth users are stoked by drug-generated paranoia. Suspicions heighten and elaborate delusions develop in which meth users believe they are being observed, followed, and in danger. Complex plots involving strangers on the street, hidden microphones and cameras, and misreading the expressions and intentions of others results in harm to both the user and those around him.

It is still unclear how long these psychotic features, if present, remain once someone has given up methamphetamine, but medical literature indicates that paranoia can persist well into abstinence. The creation of a therapeutic bond and the development of a trusting relationship are very important to move past these suspicions and help the recovering person learn to reestablish relationships in his life.

Meth's Impact on Sexual Performance

In addition to its effects on lust and behavior, meth's effects on sexual performance are, ironically, ultimately viewed by most users as extremely detrimental.

1. Meth and Sexual Duration

Many users describe having sex under the influence of methamphetamine for thirty-six or forty-eight hours. One man wrote, "When I have used meth it leads to what can only be described as a sex marathon—nonstop for hours." This duration of action of methamphetamine, sometimes up to twelve hours, is correlated with the duration of sexual activity. This is evident in this man's response: "It is the most intense high and longest lasting drug I know of. It is also cheaper in price because it lasts so long. You don't have to keep using and using to stay high. A good fat line will last twelve hours minimum." Where meth is cheap, many users acknowledge its economic advantage, but in many places around the country, including south Florida, the cost of methamphetamine now equals or is more than that of cocaine.

Ongoing meth-driven eroticism is not without its cost. Some men become obsessed with the persistent erotic force in their brains, and many can't stop trying to have sex even though physical exhaustion and dehydration set in. All other basic needs are set aside, including hunger, which is suspended by the action of the methamphetamine. Many users' lives quickly deteriorate as their exclusive focus becomes meth, sex, and more of each. Some try to satisfy their demanding sexual urges by masturbating for hours, to the point of self-injury. One man wrote, "Yes, I enjoyed the power of stamina that crystal gave me during sex, but as I grew older, I grew to want more from sex than three hours or more of mindless, useless, scraping each other raw."

2. "Crystal Dick"

One of the great ironies of methamphetamine is that, while it increases sexual pleasure, its physiological effects prevent the user from obtaining a full erection. Amphetamines constrict vessels, and a strong blood flow is needed to keep the penis erect. This inability to maintain an erection is known among gay meth users as "crystal dick." A secondary consequence of this erectile dysfunction is the *instant bottom*, a term applied to men who take a receptive role during anal intercourse because they no longer are able to "top" due to their drug use. One man wrote, "I'm pretty much a bottom due to 'difficulties' caused by meth."

In an attempt to obtain erections, many men on meth use erectile dysfunction (ED) medications, and cynically joke that the new HIV cocktail consists of methamphetamine and Viagra (sildenafil), although eventually even these ED drugs lose their effectiveness. A survey respondent reported, "After a while I couldn't get an erection, even with *Viagra*, so I became an 'instant bottom' <lol>."

Recent understanding of the brain's plasticity has shed new light on deeper causes of erectile dysfunction. With increased stimulation of sexual desire, whether through substances or behaviors such as viewing pornography, there are physical changes in the brain that will damage the ability to get an erection. This is discussed in more detail in Chapter 7, "Sex and the Plastic Brain."

3. Sensations

Almost anyone who uses meth to augment sex finds that sensations, from desire to actual sexual acts and especially anal intercourse, seem enhanced to a point never before experienced or even imagined. Many drugs increase subjective sensations during sex, but meth, at least anecdotally, seems to trump the others for sheer impact.

Increased anal sensation is commonly reported with meth, which results in a heightened probability of condomless anal intercourse,[11] the riskiest type of sex for transmission of disease. Impulsivity and disorganized thinking further reduce the likelihood of safe sex in the lust-driven moment. This sensitivity also results in more men engaging in anal sexplay such as fisting, which increases the risk of tearing the anal mucosa and exposing the individual to a variety of viruses and infections.

Increased receptive anal intercourse without safe sex practices has produced a tremendous resurgence of HIV and other sexually transmitted diseases. Dade and Broward counties in Florida, where meth use among gay men is high, rank among the highest in the country for new HIV cases and other sexually transmitted infections. This correlation between methamphetamine and new HIV infections is true in many other communities in the United States and abroad. The increased risk of exposure to HIV among meth users has been documented in a longitudinal study that followed gay men in four cities beginning in 1984.[12] When these men seroconverted, their drug habits were explored and a significant relationship was found between methamphetamine and increased HIV risk.

The sensual intensity of sex on meth becomes as addictive as the drug itself. One client, honestly believing that sober sexual experiences could never equal the meth-sex that had devastated his life, reported how the drug impacted his erotic sensations. "Sex on crystal shouldn't even be called 'sex'. Sex can never compare to the experiences I have had with crystal—it is like the 'forbidden fruit.'" Such euphoric recall, combined with the hopelessness typical of early recovery and feeling asexual without the drug, lead many men in early recovery to believe they are permanently damaged sexually.

After Meth: What Now?

It is essential that the man who uses meth or has quit using—the man who wants something better—understands the nature of his problem in order to solve it. As we have seen, meth rewires the brain, transforming desire, behavior, and sexual performance. Because of meth's insidious ability to fuse itself with sex, one of the most powerful and positive human experiences, unraveling these connections is difficult. Meth manipulates and distorts this drive until the user is forced into choosing between unbearable hopelessness and depression or pursuing even more bizarre and unobtainable fantasies. Undeterred, many meth users continue to chase the elusive sex they once had with meth until someone or something, be it a loved one, a medical diagnosis, a personal crisis, or the law, intervenes.

This pivotal point represents the "rock bottom," and it is there that many men, whose brains are deprived of mood-stabilizing neurotransmitters, become mired in hopelessness. This downward spiral begins as a thrilling grasp at intensity that infuses early experiences with methamphetamine and that predictably leads to unfortunate consequences. The next chapter examines the interplay between meth and this drive for intensity.

3

The Chase for Intensity

Kevin couldn't believe his luck. He felt himself breathing hard although he was just lying on the bed. Because the blinds were closed the bedroom was dark, but the bright daylight outside formed a luminescent square around the frame of the window. He had quickly driven over to this man's house after they hooked up online. He didn't know his real name, just his screen name. Kevin and the man he hooked up with had smoked a little tina, and the head rush was beginning to sweep him up in an erotic wave. He was beginning to feel incredibly aroused…his trick was hot…damned, Kevin felt invincible. Just as his mind was starting to run with erotic possibilities, his trick suggested that he try slamming, injecting meth, for a real powerful punch. Since Kevin arrived from Wisconsin last year he had heard of slamming but never tried it. He hadn't even tried meth until a few months ago when it was offered to him by someone at a bathhouse. But now it occurred to him that if a little smoke could do this, why not try, as his trick said, the ultimate rush?

> **Life on meth has become foreplay for the ultimate sexual experience that never happens.**
>
> — METH USER

Kevin's sexual imagination was in overdrive with this hot guy. His trick brought out the works—a syringe, some meth—Kevin

> *didn't really want to look too closely. He assured Kevin he had done this many times and never had a problem. He described slamming as the best ride of his life. Kevin got even harder. The guy prepared the syringe and sat down on the bed next to Kevin, playing with his nipples. Kevin held out his arm. This was one of the most intense moments of his life. His heart was racing with anticipation. A small voice in his head asked how he could let a stranger inject him, someone whose name he didn't know. But the excitement was building and the thrill unstoppable. As his trick broke the skin, Kevin's thrilling excitement did a twist in mid-air, a flip flop. Suddenly, even as he felt the meth hit his bloodstream and start to travel up his arm, the intensity switched from pleasurable stimulation to overwhelming anxiety. His heart raced harder—this time not from exhilaration, but from panic. In one brief moment Kevin was pulled from a thrilling ride just on this side of safety into gut churning fear. Kevin had just experienced life on a razor's edge.*

Meth frequently brings heightened drama in many forms: emotional rollercoasters, high-intensity sexual experiences, and behavior far out of bounds from "normal." Meth reduces the brain's ability to organize and judge behavior, both of which lead to considerable chaos. Deadlines pass, priorities are clouded, and problem solving remains elusive. This results in a cumulative, sharp-edged intensity that becomes self-propelling in the lives of its users. Even the unrelenting sex drive fueled by meth becomes addictive as the brain chemically adjusts to a constant state of adrenaline-spiked rush. Men crave this feeling, attempt to sustain it, and perilously walk the razor's edge between a state of boredom and being overwhelmed. The intensity itself is addictive, and the prospect of its loss, along with the lack of stimulation and idle time, represents a very serious relapse risk for those in recovery.

Meth alters the inherent balance between excitement and fearful intensity, which are actually two sides of the same coin. What is exhilarating at one moment, like Kevin's thrilling surrender to a stranger injecting him with meth, quickly turns to panic as the potentially fatal consequences of reckless thrill-seeking become conscious. Yet despite the terrifying, electrical sparks of panic that are triggered, meth's ability to seduce the user with the promise of thrilling excitement and new sensations literally overwhelms caution and good judgment.

In his book *The Dangerous Edge: The Psychology of Excitement*,[1] Michael Apter presents a model for understanding excitement as a natural element of human existence. Whether or not these edgy and thrilling experiences are considered pleasant or unpleasant depends on the individual's "protective frame." This frame is a person's subjective belief that he will not actually go over the dangerous edge but remain safe, just on this side of disaster. This protective frame is highly variable among individuals and is the result of numerous factors such as personal confidence, availability of others to help, the presence of physical aids, and the accumulation of life experiences. Meth use drives excitement through high-risk sex, a sense of danger, or even allowing a stranger to inject meth into one's arm. This is similar to individuals who pursue high-risk activities such as mountain climbing or bungee jumping in order to get as close as possible to the dangerous edge while still operating within their personal protective frame. The result is a very stimulating, if risky, experience. Meth, with its power to reduce inhibitions and bolster confidence, shifts an individual's protective frame, resulting in risky behaviors that may be totally uncharacteristic for the user.

It is not unusual for someone experiencing excitement (high arousal and pleasant feelings) to suddenly undergo a reversal of mood if the situation changes, rapidly shifting from pleasurable stimulation to anxiety (high arousal and unpleasant feelings). There are countless circumstances when this might occur. Kevin experienced such a shift when a stranger plunged a syringe into his arm. Another man might panic as he finds himself in a bondage scene quickly evolving beyond his personal limits. Someone else who might be enjoying an intense connection involving anal intercourse could quickly panic should the condom suddenly break. In each of these circumstances the individual experiences a rapid reversal from excitement to anxiety, quickly breaking the erotic spell.

Four very different emotional states can be plotted using Apter's "dangerous edge" concept, combining low and high levels of arousal with pleasant and unpleasant feelings. 1) High levels of arousal combined with pleasant feelings results in excitement, a state constantly sought by someone chasing a meth high. 2) High arousal combined with more unpleasant feelings, on the other hand, results in a heightened state of anxiety, something every meth user has experienced. 3) Low levels of arousal combined with pleasant feelings translates into relaxation, while, 4) low levels of arousal combined with unpleasant feelings results in boredom.

Meth users abhor low levels of arousal and unpleasant feelings. Many addicts seek to numb emotional pain, loneliness, boredom, low self-esteem, and a host of other uncomfortable feelings...but meth users in particular seem to become particularly intolerant of them. As one's meth use progresses, such feelings become more and more intolerable, and the urge to escape them becomes ever greater. Low levels of stimulation are equally uncomfortable for a meth user, with boredom being one of the most powerful relapse triggers. Many people who stop using meth (and other drugs) find that a great deal of energy and time that had been directed toward thinking about, acquiring, using, and recovering from drugs is now available, often with no specific productive focus. Such "open space" is fertile ground for cravings or rationalizations that quickly undermine efforts to stay clean. One easy solution in such cases is to fill that time with support groups and recovery-related activities.

It is thus essential for someone in recovery to learn ways to manage their feelings and to increase their ability to tolerate periods of low stimulation. The same is true for people with Attention Deficit Hyperactivity Disorder, who, research[2] shows, have fewer dopamine receptors and therefore find "normal" levels of stimulation dull and painfully boring.

Anyone seeking heightened arousal quickly learns that combining several stimulating behaviors synergistically creates even more intensity and excitement. Stated simply, stacking arousal sources has a cumulative effect. Sexuality provides countless ways that arousal sources can be combined for effect. Meth used with other drugs, of course, frequently enhances a sexual experience. Other elements that evoke a heightened level of excitement include emotions like anger, something to add novelty (such as a new sexual position or fetish), or even new sex partners.

Another major source of synergistic excitement used by gay men both on and off methamphetamine is the unique thrill associated with breaking taboos: violating rules or societal expectations. Many gay men admit experiencing the thrill associated with sexual transgression. Crossing social or moral boundaries heightens arousal and, combined with the disinhibiting qualities of meth, quickly pulls the user into outrageous behavior that, often for the first time in his life, makes a man feel, as one of my clients stated, "defiantly proud to be gay." The urge to exhibit genuine pride is, of course, positive, but facilitating its expression through risky behavior fueled by meth or other drugs is ultimately a destructive course of action. The significance of taboo among gay men using meth is discussed more completely in the next section on sexual desire.

Meth use often does not occur in isolation, but with other drugs and behaviors dependent on the context of the moment. For example, meth use at a dance venue frequently involves "club" drugs, often known as the alphabet drugs because they are referred to by the first letter of their name (X or ecstasy, G or gamma hydroxybutyrate, and K or ketamine). Sexual encounters with meth frequently result in erectile dysfunction, so medications to treat those symptoms may be used as well. Sedatives may also be ingested to calm the user after an extended high, or to settle a frazzled nervous system after days of drug use. Drugs and behaviors that frequently occur in combination with meth are described below.

Sex Addiction, Pornography, and Cybersex

Meth energizes hypersexuality in gay men to the point that many become consumed with the process of thinking about sex, obsessively planning sexual encounters, having sex, and even obsessing about the next sexual encounter before the current liaison is complete. This compulsive behavior has another name—sex addiction. Not every sex addict is a meth user, but most gay meth users become sex addicts.

The concept of sex addiction has been controversial among professionals because some have conceptualized addiction exclusively in terms of substances ingested into the body to achieve an altered state. They believe that other behaviors such as sex, gambling, exercise, overeating, and even shopping are certainly compulsive, but cannot appropriately be labeled addiction.

As the science of brain function evolves, it has become clear that certain behaviors, in addition to drugs, cause chemical changes that are indeed addictive because they are progressive and because tolerance develops, meaning a state where more of the behavior is needed to achieve the same result. Behavior-induced alterations of mood, such as compulsive gambling or binge eating, are considered to be *process* addictions as opposed to substance-induced alterations of mood.

The effects of sex while on methamphetamine and sex addiction are frequently indistinguishable. It is important for someone recovering from meth to be familiar with lessons learned from sex addiction. Much of the groundbreaking work in sex addiction has been done by Patrick Carnes, who has published numerous articles and books on the subject.[3] Carnes found that many sex addicts (83 percent) have other addictions, or co-occurring disorders, including substance abuse (42 percent), eating disorders (38 percent), compulsive working (28 percent), compulsive spending (26 percent), and compulsive gambling (5 percent).[4]

Carnes found that sexual addiction mirrors substance-use disorders in several ways. There is a loss of control indicated by a persistent desire or unsuccessful efforts to control or stop the sexual behaviors. There is a continuation of the behavior despite adverse consequences. Finally, there is an obsession or preoccupation with obtaining, using, or recovering from the behavior. Significantly, Carnes and others have observed that sexual addiction is not a replacement for substance addiction and does not cause it (as many believe) due to decreased inhibition when intoxicated, but rather that the two are separate co-occurring illnesses.

Gay men may be at increased risk of such compulsive sexual behavior due to higher rates of impulse control disorders than are observed among the general population. In a study that was part of the National Health and Social Life Survey,[5] researchers found that, among a treatment population, 50 percent of gay or bisexual men reported a problem with current compulsive sexual behavior, as opposed to 9.6 percent of the heterosexual men studied. Nearly 60 percent of the gay or bisexual men in the study reported a problem with compulsive sexual behavior during their lifetime, compared to 10 percent of the heterosexual study population. The study also found that gay men were more prone to other impulse control disorders such as compulsive gambling and compulsive shopping.

Sex addicts often share characteristics related to their family of origin, such as multiple addictive and/or compulsive disorders. Among adults who experienced dysfunction at an early age, there is sometimes an inability to sustain intimacy in relationships due to a failure to trust others enough to form a bond with them, as well as a rigid and authoritarian personality, resulting in resistance to accountability. One client named Scott grew up in an evangelical home with very specific and strict beliefs about religion, morality, and sexuality. Unable to reconcile his sexual orientation or provide sufficient self-soothing for other uncomfortable emotions, Scott deferred to the dictates of a few people of authority around him. Over time, this rigidity spilled over into every area of Scott's life as he readily rejected dissonant thoughts or ideas. He seethed with suppressed hostility and indirectly expressed his rage through passive aggressive behavior and sexually "acting out" with numerous, anonymous encounters.

A variety of other factors may lead to compulsive sexual behavior. These include childhood abuse, significant losses of primary caregivers, an enmeshed relationship with a parent, exposure to inappropriate sexual information or behaviors, or some other form of trauma. Some individuals who exhibit compulsive sexual behavior while under the influence of methamphetamine may not share these risk characteristics in their profile, but as a result of their use of the drug, exhibit behavior similar to those with such histories.

One factor common to both sexual addicts and those ingesting meth is that both use sex as a mood changer to mask emotional pain. Sex ultimately becomes less about erotic desire and more directed toward avoiding emotional pain through the manipulation of the pain-killing effects of dopamine and other neurotransmitters. The major challenge of recovery from either (or both) is learning how to experience, in a healthy way, the various emotions that bubble up once the numbing effects have worn off.

Both sex and meth addiction can be conceptualized as intimacy disorders.[6] They compensate for the inability of an individual to adequately bond in intimate relationships, and indeed may cause or worsen any intimacy concerns that are present. The ultimate treatment goal for sex addiction, as with meth addiction, is "mastering the experience of forming enduring and trusting intimate connections with others,"[7] and, I would add, an intimate connection with oneself. The most common barriers preventing addicts from achieving these intimate connections include shame, the inability to self-regulate emotions, and not maintaining sexual boundaries.

Despite the toll extracted by sex addiction, gay social norms continue to minimize, if not actually glorify, over-the-top sexual behavior. Numerous advertisements in local gay magazines are highly sexualized and, at times, celebrate reckless, irresponsible, and defiant behavior in a way that is damaging to gay men. This criticism does not derive from a prudish or rigid attitude about sex, but from witnessing the harm done to countless gay men who succumbed to the exhilaration of unbound sex and paid a huge price with their physical and emotional health.

Pornography is a familiar companion in the lives of men driven by sex and drugs. Many men describe "meth runs" that last four or five days, the entire duration of which is filled with heightened sexual energy. When not actually engaged in sex, men use porn to sustain a sexually-charged, drug-induced trance. Porn, like meth, has a powerful impact on the fantasies of erotic desire. Both affect the mind, and it is through endless hours spent watching porn that men stumble across new fantasies or sexual positions that fire up long-buried or undiscovered erotic scripts. These almost always evolve, moving quickly from mundane vanilla sex to darker themes, revealing the shadow selves of the men.

One of my clients who sought assistance in quitting meth was also a gay porn star and producer. His videos were among those exhibiting bareback sex, and he aspired to further develop his films by incorporating more elaborate plot lines, rarely seen (or sought, for that matter) in gay porn. Because they included developed characters, I suggested how valuable it would be for one of them to be a recovering meth addict. I felt this had great potential to serve as an influential role model to his viewers. He rejected this out of hand, noting that although he himself had been nearly destroyed by meth, he understood that a significant percentage of his audience was high on the drug when viewing his films, and including such a recovering character would be the ultimate "buzz kill," breaking the erotic spell of the porn.

Pornography, with or without meth, is subject to the psychological principle of habituation, where tolerance to the source of stimulation develops. The level of erotic arousal response decreases with repetition. Simply put, the stimulating effects quickly diminish with repeated viewings, resulting in a short "shelf-life" for porn. There is also a kind of "kink-creep" that occurs, and this is frequently seen among meth users. What was stimulating yesterday is boring today, and something a little more exotic is needed to achieve the desired level of sexual arousal. Soon, even that becomes less interesting, and something kinkier may be pursued. With the passage of time, interest in vanilla sex will be extinguished and increasing levels of stimulus will be required. This frequently involves fantasies involving power, exploitation, and even aggression that many individuals find disturbing. It also victimizes partners of porn addicts, for whom the addict loses interest, becoming an unwelcome third party, excluded from the erotic bond between the addict and his fantasies.

Habituation also results in numbing the individual to acts of violence, both sexual and non-sexual. While there is a distinct difference between sexual fantasy and sexual acting out that most people clearly recognize, a small minority of individuals, especially under the influence of methamphetamine and other drugs, will merge fantasy and reality in their behavior. This is further complicated by the psychotic features that sometimes accompany the use of methamphetamine.

Pornography sparks strong feelings and can be seen as a barometer of societal tolerance. Photographs, videos, and written erotica have long had a dual relationship with society: at once reviled and for many, secretly pursued. Some defend it while others point out the cost of pornography, including promoting objectification of the individuals portrayed. Methamphetamine, by reducing empathy, only reinforces exploitation and objectification. The objectification of homosexual men in pornography does not provoke the resentment among gay men that is often experienced about women portrayed in a pornographic context. Many gay men joke that they would like to be a porn star and among some this represents socially sanctioned behavior. Most gay men reading such ads probably do not consider its negative effects as such behavior increasingly becomes the social norm.

The Internet has made access to pornography inexpensive, nearly universal, and very private, resulting in a virtual explosion of porn as people pursue erotic interests in the privacy of their own homes. Sexually explicit materials no doubt represent a significant portion of traffic on the Internet, and the resulting variety, quantity, and availability of pornographic material is truly astounding.

Many people joke that if there is a fetish, no matter how obscure, there is probably an Internet site or blog devoted to it. In one sense, this serves a positive purpose. Isolated individuals who share an interest in a particular fetish once had to find each other, which was no easy task. This most often occurred in larger cities where the chances of encountering someone else with similar tastes were significantly greater. Fetishes have been stigmatized by society at large, resulting in a good deal of furtiveness and shame among those who weren't comfortable with their own desires.

The Internet has allowed people to discover others with like-minded tastes around the world and communicate with them with relative ease. Cyber-communities of various fetishists thrive. This communication has allowed some to discover that they are not alone with their thoughts and fantasies, and, for the first time, they can break their relative isolation rather easily. For these people the Internet and its "pornography" have served a positive purpose in helping them move past isolation, fear, and shame while exploring their feelings.

On the other hand, the ease with which one shares pictures and video content feeds some of the negative aspects of meth addiction. Visual stimuli are particularly potent for someone using meth. One study at UCLA[8] found that even months after using meth for the last time, the visual memory of recovering individuals functioned significantly better than verbal memory. That is, visual images were more clearly grasped and retained by the brain than were words or abstract statements. These visual properties serve as powerful triggers for the drug and reinforce various rituals of use, such as slamming meth (injecting it intravenously). This is true for other drugs to some extent as well, and has practical application for relapse prevention. As a young clinician I worked in an inpatient treatment center in Florida during the height of the cocaine epidemic in the late 1980s. At that time we had less understanding of the visual impact of certain images on drug users, and we screened educational videos depicting the drugs and users' works (needles and pipes). Our patients became increasingly uncomfortable and some would flee the room. They were experiencing cravings brought on by the visual images. Such effects are not limited to images. Many clients have expressed distress caused by walking into a twelve-step room, or by seeing and hearing other addicts share their experiences.

Visual appeal is found in certain meth-related web-based video chat communities that have "slammer rooms" where meth users around the world can watch each other inject meth. The visual image of someone injecting themselves or being injected becomes linked (or generalized) to the subjective sensation of the effects of methamphetamine, and serves as a stimulus that quickly pushes the viewer to the razor's edge. These visual links to the sensation of intoxication become especially burdensome when someone attempts to quit meth and finds that visual stimuli in everyday life brings on a strong craving for the drug.

In addition to pornographic material, the Internet has played a key role in the distribution and popularity of methamphetamine. A variety of social networking Internet sites and apps designed to enable sexual liaisons have emerged that have revolutionized the concept of gay cruising. Men can, as one site boasts, "log on and get off." In Fort Lauderdale, which has a large gay tourist industry, visitors arrive and within a few moments of checking into their hotel or guesthouse log on to find a sex partner. This frequently means finding someone to share drugs, as well, known as "party and play" (PNP).

Profiles are posted with photographs or video clips, personal statements, and even categories of sexual roles and interests. Users can quickly sort through a database and find potential sex partners in virtually any corner of the world. Codes have emerged that allow cruisers to specifically sort for a sex partner who also is amenable to using drugs, or not. Profiles refer to "PNP" or "no PNP," which stands for "party and play" or "no party and play." Sometimes the term "chem friendly" is also used to denote someone who does not object to the use of drugs during sexual encounters. Some men convey an interest in meth in a more codified form, such as "let me be crystal clear," or "let's get to the point" (a reference to syringes and slamming).

The use of such terminology has not been lost on law enforcement officers who, in some cities, post profiles on these sites indicating an interest in PNP. One client of mine arranged to meet someone with whom he chatted on a sex site. The man promised to have drugs, but when my client arrived at the rendezvous site he was arrested by the police. The legal issue of entrapment in such cases remains undetermined.

Drug use has also had an impact on one of the central venues of gay social life: bars and clubs. Dance clubs, in particular, have struggled as alcohol sales have declined. While club drugs and alcohol don't mix well, another liquid is necessary for hydration when these drugs are consumed: water. In some areas, gay clubs have found the demand for water outpacing that for alcoholic beverages. The Internet is now playing such a large role in gay social interaction that many venues like these dance clubs are struggling to survive. As a cover story in the

Leather Journal noted a few years ago, "let's get leathermen off their computers and back into the bars like the good old days."

The Internet and the rise of various social apps to find partners have changed how gay men hook up, the distribution of meth and other drugs, and the very survival of bars and clubs. Men no longer find it necessary to go out to dance venues or a bar to hook up either for drugs or sex. Hundreds of potential sexual partners are quickly, efficiently, and easily screened from one's home computer or mobile device. With a few instant messages back and forth, time and place are quickly arranged, and the encounter begins. Like motels stranded on old highways bypassed by the interstates, clubs have had to work harder to attract and retain their gay clientele, and some have not survived. Fort Lauderdale, for example, had five or six gay dance clubs several years ago, and now only a few remain. The *Village Voice* reports[9] that in New York in the '80s, three thousand members were packing the Saint for eighteen-hour marathons. By 2002, up to two thousand men were dancing into Sunday morning at the Roxy, and by 2012 the city's only dedicated gay dance club, XL, had an official capacity of seven hundred fifty. Gay men will always want to congregate, dance, and experience the collective energy of such a locale, but the necessity of such clubs for cruising and drug connections has given way to the information age.

Cross-Addiction and Relapse Risk

When multiple substances or behaviors are involved it is known as cross-addiction. This concept is particularly important for someone considering or attempting recovery. The central role of denial and bargaining in addiction makes it easy for someone to convince themselves that methamphetamine or some other specific drug or group of drugs is the problem, but that alcohol, sedatives and pain killers, compulsive sex, gambling, or shopping can all be safely managed. This is dangerous thinking because it maintains the notion that relief of unpleasant feelings is found in a chemical or behavior. It also keeps the brain in a state of craving for relief and greatly increases the chance of relapse.

The experience of many persons in recovery shows that complete abstinence from the addictive substances or behaviors is the best, if not the only, solution for recovery. As long as an addictive "back door" outlet remains active, real recovery in physical, emotional, and sexual terms will remain elusive.

The greatest danger of cross-addiction, then, is its threat to overall recovery. The influence of one addictive behavior can result in the addict losing control of his thoughts and behaviors and ultimately returning to his original drug of choice. Terry Gorski,[10] a pioneer in the field of relapse prevention, describes the relapse process as one similar to knocking over a row of dominoes. The first hits the second, the second hits the third, and so on until the process goes full circle and one is crushed by a gigantic domino at the end of this chain. Relapse prevention is about learning how to avoid tipping over the first domino and developing strategies for stopping the chain reaction should that occur.

Cross-addiction plays a significant role in this relapse process simply because there are so many opportunities to push over the first domino. As pain or stress in recovery is inevitably encountered, the addict may turn to other compulsive behaviors such as sex, work, and even dysfunctional relationships to soothe emotional discomfort. While this may temporarily relieve unpleasant feelings, the core issue persists, and the stress and emotional pain return. Eventually, the cumulative toll of these stressors and the use of other compulsive behaviors snowballs into a major relapse. As Gorski says, "relapse always grows from the inside out."

The context in which meth use occurs is critically important in order to understand why the drug is used, by whom, and for what purpose. The role of other drugs or co-occurring compulsive behaviors such as sex must also be acknowledged if one hopes to curtail the damaging effects on individuals, families, and the community. The next chapter concludes Part I, explaining how HIV, meth, and its use by gay men have created the perfect storm.

4

Men, Drugs, and a Deadly Virus

Like all drugs that rise in popularity, peak, and then succumb to the growing appeal of something else, methamphetamine has impacted the gay community in several waves. In the United States, it began in Hawaii, and became a staple of some gay communities on the West Coast in the 1980s and 1990s. This progression was amplified by circuit parties and the high level of travel among gay men, and by 2002, the drug was fully embedded in gay life across the country.

> **I was healthy before I met Tina—now my life has been changed forever.**
>
> —METH USER

Following the 2006 enactment of federal regulations controlling its precursor pseudoephedrine, there was an initial drop in use. After a lull of several years, however, meth made another surge in popularity, this time supplied by Mexican-manufactured drugs that had very high purity and lower prices. By 2012, the drug was once again snaring men who escaped the first wave, had come of age since then, or who had successfully resisted earlier temptation. Early warning signs were limited to therapists' offices and Crystal Meth Anonymous meetings, but epidemiological data finally began to capture the trend after 2013.

Meth seems to be a "perfect storm" for the gay community, coming at a time of heightened cultural divisions about civil rights for same-sex persons, weariness of the AIDS crisis that has persisted more than thirty years, a new generation of gay men who did not experience the health-related losses of an earlier generation, and the seduction of a powerful, sex-enhancing drug.

It is counterproductive to damn methamphetamine, although it has few redeeming qualities, or to demonize the men who use it, simply because such pronouncements provide no solutions and result in little except more stigma and shame. A more useful approach is to understand the complex relationship between gay men and substances, including methamphetamine, by looking at the role such drugs play for the individual, his social networks, and the community at large.

Susceptible Men

I have found it useful to distinguish between casual (or low intensity) users and binge (or high intensity) users who consume the drug in greater amounts and with higher frequency. Low frequency users seem to be able to control their use, or even walk away from the drug when they feel it is getting the upper hand. They seek the effect of the drug to enhance sex, complete tasks, and increase their waking hours for work or study. In my experience, everyone *wants* to be a casual user who remains free of significant problems while accepting short-term consequences such as feeling washed-out for several days. The majority of men seeking assistance, however, report that they quickly lose control over meth and become binge or high intensity users. With astonishing speed, many report having lost jobs, partners, homes, money, and health.

Denial as it pertains to addiction is well understood. It may be true that there are people who use meth socially without consequences. It is also true that virtually all of the people I see who have plunged into big trouble with meth were, at one time, social users who felt that meth was a recreational addition to their lives that they could easily control. For many, denial was a factor in slipping further down a dangerous slope, making the climb out much more difficult. As this progression occurred, many did not realize the full impact of the drug on their lives. They minimized and rationalized their drug use, attempting to impose controls on their consumption and personal behavior while under the influence.

Slowly, and for others much more quickly, meth began to creep out of its social confines and consume more and more of their daily lives. They describe intense sex on the drug, and many who had experienced chronic low energy and/or felt mildly depressed for years found themselves able to do things they simply weren't motivated to do before. These individuals began to use meth, often in combination with other drugs, with greater frequency. Weekend use spilled over into Monday when they called in sick to their jobs. This rolled over into the next day, sometimes called "suicide Tuesday" because of the depression that follows several days of meth use. Frequently, weekend partying started on Thursday, or even Wednesday. Suddenly, many of these users found themselves caught in a swirling vortex from which they were unable to break free.

Methamphetamine has a high potential for abuse and its physical effects are severe and long lasting. It creates an intense euphoria followed by an equally intense, sometimes suicidal depression. While the speed of meth's addictive potential may be argued, most experts agree it is an extremely dangerous drug. How can this drug hold such appeal? Despite its obvious negative consequences, for certain gay men, this drug creates an illusory cure for ongoing concerns: escaping emotional pain, breaking through inhibitions, stoking sexual desire, and finding a social identity.

Escaping Emotional Pain

"I feel like damaged goods." I first heard these painful words from clients who were trying to dig out from under stigma and shame. It has certainly become easier to grow up gay in America, but the sustained high rates of addiction and suicide in the LGBT population indicate that there is still considerable stress involved in coming to terms with being gay. Over the past decade I have consistently heard these words from men in individual therapy, in groups, in trainings, and in every area of the United States.

This persistent stigma comes from outside of oneself and is expressed in discrimination, alienation, violence, or marginalization. It also, however, is an "inside job," or what is called "felt stigma." As a means of self-protection, one becomes hyperalert to potential stigma, resulting in internalized feelings of fear and shame. These pressures, along with a host of other factors, dramatically increases one's vulnerability to high-risk sexual acts that result in exposure to HIV, hepatitis, and many other health concerns and increased substance use. Those who are already infected also experience "felt stigma" in the US where, in 2012, one quarter of American adults believed they could "catch" AIDS from sharing drinking cups or household objects.[1]

Being both gay and HIV-positive brings a host of other concerns. I know many men who have lived with HIV/AIDS for several decades and who, although relatively healthy, are experiencing its long-term effects. They feel isolated, unattractive, invisible, and sexually impaired—in brief, like damaged goods. A drug like methamphetamine places these men in a dilemma. While most are aware of its damaging effects, they also find that it neutralizes these negative feelings. It empowers, fuels sexuality, disinhibits, and makes them feel like they belong.

The function of methamphetamine and other drugs as a tool to control psychological symptoms remains an understudied, yet significant factor in determining differences between those who use infrequently versus those who use the drug chronically. One study[2] found that the reasons a particular gay man uses methamphetamine are significant in predicting how much and how frequently he uses the drug. Chronic users were found to use the drug more as a coping strategy to deal with uncomfortable feelings, physical pain, and as a tool to engage in pleasant times than those who were occasional binge users.

Breaking through Inhibitions

The emotional resilience of millions of gay men who become healthy, strong, and productive members of the community in the face of bias, discrimination, and even hatred is truly remarkable. Sometimes against all odds, gay men display astounding inherent strength in defining, expressing, and often redefining themselves.

This process, however, is not an easy one, and universal concerns such as shyness and inhibition take on special meaning for many gay men struggling to be true to themselves in the face of heightened judgment both from within and from others. For many, the essence of this struggle is overcoming the learned shame that has confined them for most of their lives. A great number of gay men have become accustomed to keeping portions of themselves that they deem socially unacceptable hidden, sometimes even in the company of other gay men.

Many find that social inhibition becomes a growing problem. Gay men, particularly those who are middle aged or older, frequently lack the experience of social rehearsal, dating, and development of intimacy skills that is the norm for heterosexuals in our society. The developmental experiences they have had in these areas are often lubricated by alcohol and other mood-altering drugs. It is not uncommon, for example, for my gay clients never to have had sex unless under the influence of a substance.

Methamphetamine is particularly effective at banishing social and sexual inhibition, offering chemical courage combined with impaired judgment that has resulted in the oft-cited statistics about growing rates of HIV associated with meth use. This is not a new phenomenon. Many generations of gay men have described using alcohol or other drugs to obliterate concerns and act out on their sexual impulses. Meth serves this function as well, helping them overcome negative social meanings of being gay. For others, however, meth doesn't just neutralize negative feelings about being gay, it promotes the feeling of resolute determination and pride about one's sexual feelings, a sensation that initially is profoundly affirming. One survey respondent from Long Beach, California, noted that, "where other drugs (alcohol, cocaine, LSD) used to help me hide from my sexuality, meth finally made it be okay to be gay."

However, there is increasing stigma surrounding men who use meth within the gay community itself. Like society at large, many men who don't use crystal meth are critical of those who do. Sometimes they express empathy, but often verbalize disgust, as well. Those making such judgments don't realize the polarizing effects.

To help gay men successfully avoid meth and its powerful ability to disinhibit, it is important to acknowledge the need of gay men to connect to each other on a variety of levels. They need to embrace their similarities and honor and support each other. Only by addressing their own internalized shame, as well as that of the community at large, will they be able to undermine the web of social and emotional concerns that make some gay men vulnerable to meth.

Stoking Sexual Desire

I occasionally treat a man who used meth for energy or to lose weight and either didn't realize the sexual potential of methamphetamine or was never able to connect the drug's effects with his sexual feelings. Such men are often resentful that the sexual effects of meth eluded them. Many men and women around the world use the drug for its energizing characteristics: long haul truckers, migrant farm workers, domestic workers, factory workers in the third world, oil rig workers, and even soccer moms. But in the gay universe, the majority of men have crosswired the dopamine-charged feelings of invincibility and power with sexual desire.

One client explained this aptly, "I was a sex maniac on the drug—I never wanted the sex to end, ever." These words from a man using meth capture the most significant factor related to its use among gay men. The drug boosts sexual desire to an almost torturous level. Sexual urges become paramount and rational thought (particularly concerning safer sex) becomes largely irrelevant. For many gay men who have suffered a degree of shame concerning sex, the supercharged sexual desire created by meth is a fantastic release from a judgmental superego that held them captive their entire adult lives. For other men, particularly those who are older, those who have lived with HIV for many years, or those who (for whatever reason) infrequently feel strong sexual desire, meth delivers a temporary sexual surge that seems to turn back the body's physiological clock.

What could be the downside of turbulent sexual desire? There are, of course, many, but several are key. Perhaps most significant is that rational thought is minimized when the reward center of the brain is in control. This means that all internalized knowledge about HIV prevention and safer sex, and all the years of vigilance about protected sex can be discarded with a single hit of meth. Most users report that the drug makes them complacent, whether about paying their bills, showing up for work, or particularly, slowing down the sexual intensity of the moment to be safe. For this very reason, meth is a critical factor in the ongoing high rates of HIV infection among gay men, as well as runaway epidemics of other sexually transmitted diseases.

There is another downside to super-stimulated sexual desire. Methamphetamine affects anticipatory desire, the phase of sexual desire that leads up to the physiological climax. Under normal circumstances, an orgasm, in addition to physiological release, will relieve desire, at least during the so-called refractory period after climax. This is the phase—generally at least thirty minutes—during which the body recovers and during which another orgasm is physiologically impossible. Many men who use meth often describe no such effect. While it is impossible for them to achieve an erection, they continue to experience a relentless sexual drive long after their bodies are no longer capable of ongoing sexual activity.

Finding a Social Identity

Sex has often played a role as a social leveler in both gay and straight societies. It is often true that one's sexual community may not be the same as one's social community. Many gay men lust for men for whom there is no emotional connection. Sex brings together men of wildly different socio-economic, ethnic, or racial backgrounds. It levels the sexual playing field, at least temporarily, and breaks down boundaries. Various sexual fetishes and tastes unite men who might not encounter each other in other circumstances. A taste for bondage, for example, brings together men of diverse backgrounds and overcomes other social barriers. Sex gives a young man entrance to social worlds he would normally not access. Many ethnic minority gay men in New York have discovered that the sex and drug culture around methamphetamine allows them quick access to mainstream gay culture in the city. This comes at a price, as it is often accompanied by some form of exploitation because, while a different world may be accessible, the power differential between the two remains.

Sex is divisive as well. HIV status has resulted in a rift within the gay community that continues to play a significant role in how gay men see themselves and the society to which they belong. The practice of serosorting has been a significant aspect of selecting partners. The approval of the HIV drug Truvada to be used as pre-exposure prophylaxis (PrEP) has lessened the significance of serostatus, although many HIV-positive men still prefer to only date other HIV-positive men, believing this reduces the stress caused by a lack of shared experience and anxiety over infecting one's partner. Personal ads often explicitly note the HIV status of the person placing the ad and that of the desired partner. This is often expressed within a profile in a succinct and dismissively offensive shorthand: "HIV— UB2" or "disease free—UB2." On the other hand, many men who are HIV-negative express a concern that they have been "left out" in the great push within the gay community to care for our HIV-positive brothers and provide services and support systems. They feel excluded because the attention of a generation has been focused on the needs of only part of their community.

In much the same way as sex, drugs (including alcohol) are a pervasive and definitive aspect of gay identity. Many believe this is because bars were the social centers where gay men meet one another. Many gay social transactions occur in the context of alcohol. With the popularity of sexual networking sites on the Internet, many sexual transactions have moved to the cyberworld. It is extremely easy to hook up, both sexually and to party with drugs.

An Ominous Drug

Methamphetamine, many say, is the "drug du jour" currently having its day. Many hope that its luster shall soon pass, only to be replaced by another drug. Others point to an unnecessary hysteria about meth, fueled by articles in the press that sensationalize its effects. They cite films such as the 1936 classic "Reefer Madness," in which the effects of marijuana were over-stated to the point of comedy. They feel that people have cried wolf too many times about the dangers of drugs, and about this drug in particular. Still others, including most of the media, report that meth is instantly addictive and that there is no cure, insisting that meth users are doomed to a life of relapse, misery, and ultimately death. While this contributes to a sense of hopelessness, there are clear paths to recovery.

In his book, *Drug, Set, and Setting*, Norman Zinberg[3] described several factors that must be taken into account when considering the use of an illicit drug. The first of these is the drug itself, along with its inherent psychopharmacological properties. Meth does indeed electrify the part of the brain that makes behaviors such as sex extremely rewarding. This is seen in the experiences of countless users, as well as the correlation of methamphetamine use among gay men with the consequent rise in rates of HIV infection rates and other sexually transmitted diseases such as syphilis, gonorrhea, and Hepatitis B and Hepatitis C.

Despite its ability to foment sexual arousal, methamphetamine has other noted properties. It creates a boost of energy that appears to heighten awareness, makes sleep unessential, reduces appetite, and gives the user the ability to complete often mundane tasks like housework or, as in the case of one client, to stock grocery shelves all night long without "going out of his mind." Methamphetamine has been famously used by long-haul truckers to keep them awake as they drive their rigs across the country. In south Florida, migrant farm workers use methamphetamine to get through long days picking produce in hot fields. In Miami, immigrant women, many from Central America, use meth to work two or three jobs each day as domestic workers, cleaning and caring for their employer's children.

Meth is not just an issue in the US. In Asia, particularly, meth has become a social concern. Workers in Thailand, for example, commonly ingest a methamphetamine in pill form called yaba, which means "crazy medicine" in Thai, in order to work long hours. Predictably, this has resulted in a drop in productivity as the drug begins to dominate the user's lives. It fuels Thailand's sex industry and has become a huge social problem to which the Thai government has responded with severe measures in an effort to get drug use under control.

Methamphetamine was used by all sides in World War II, the Japanese, the Germans, and the Allies. It is said kamikaze pilots used meth, and it is known that US soldiers were given five amphetamine tablets in their basic kits. According to his personal physician's diaries, Hitler was addicted to methamphetamine, injecting it daily. This may explain not only some of Hitler's physical tremors that were noted toward the end of his life, but also the increased paranoia and disorganized thinking that was reported toward the end of the war as he barricaded himself in his bunker.

In the glory days of the suburban 1950s in the United States, pharmaceutical companies marketed drugs containing methamphetamine as a cure-all for depression, anxiety, and the "monotonous and tedious tasks of today's housewife."

Zinberg's second factor as to what compels someone to use a drug and how it affects them is "mindset," the attitude of the person at the time of use, including his personality structure. If a trucker is using the drug to stay awake for seventy-two hours, he will associate that drug with a boost in wakefulness. Sexual thoughts may be part of the "set" for the trucker, but often his first association with meth will be energy and not sex.

For gay men, the mindset most often associated with meth centers on sex, which itself is central to gay identity. After years spent repressing homosexual thoughts and desires, many gay men come out of the closet with a bang. Any gay newspaper or magazine emphasizes the sexual element of the culture. While this seems to reinforce the simplistic stereotype that gay men think of nothing but sex, it is actually more subtle, and the phenomenon is seen in straight culture as well. Sex pervades marketing for clothes, beer, automobiles, even insurance. Specialized gay travel promises exotic sexual experiences, or at least the possibility to observe such experiences. Gay culture values youth, sexual prowess, and symbols of prestige. This sexual "mindset" for methamphetamine among gay men, because of the drug's characteristics and the psychological susceptibility noted above, leads to devastating consequences for both the individual and the community.

Zinberg's final element is "social setting," the influence of the physical and social setting in which the using occurs. The inherent stigma of gay life, the social disconnection felt by many gay men, the wide-ranging and social acceptability of shaming homosexuality, and the ominous shadow of the HIV epidemic have all contributed to the appeal of methamphetamine among gay men.

Thus far we have examined two elements of this perfect storm: the concerns of some gay men in light of personal and social pressures, and the powerful psychopharmacology of methamphetamine itself. The final element of this triad is HIV.

Human Immunodeficiency Virus

Many studies have documented the association between meth use and the rise of HIV.[4,5] In south Florida, where there is a large gay community, there has been a significant history of meth use as well as consistently alarming rates of new infections. Broward, Dade, and Palm Beach counties have some of the highest rates of seroconversion, or new HIV infections, in the country.

Besides the risk of HIV, there are serious consequences for people who are already positive and who use crystal meth. As noted earlier, many men who are long-term survivors of HIV and who are in their forties and fifties, turn to meth as a way to instantly make themselves feel attractive, energized, and sexual.

Some men use methamphetamine to manage symptoms of their HIV. Robinson and Rempel[6] found that men have used meth to treat HIV-related depression, fatigue, and neuropathic pain. HIV-related diarrhea also seemed to diminish with meth use, but this did not appear to be a motivation for the meth use.

Men who have sex with men (MSM), African-American women, and injection drug users (IDU) are the populations most at risk of HIV exposure. Little is known about infection rates between MSM who are IDU versus MSM who are not IDU. Researchers at the Centers for Disease Control and Prevention studied these populations and found that MSM who were also IDU reported having sex with more women and identifying themselves more as "barebackers," or men who intentionally have condomless anal intercourse. Although injection drug users reported more unprotected sexual behavior than men who did not use drugs at all, their sexual risk behaviors were similar to men who used non-injection drugs. Injection drug users also reported more polydrug use, including meth, amphetamines, barbiturates, and gamma hydroxybutyrate (GBH).

One major concern about the intersection of meth and HIV is antiretroviral medication adherence. Medical professionals have long reported poor adherence among those using recreational drugs. Many gay men using meth report "planned non-adherence." That is, they know that they will be unable to take their meds as prescribed over a party weekend, so they just stop taking them for a few days. This, of course, results in the development of resistance to medications, significantly or totally reducing their effectiveness for fighting HIV. Other men employ a strategy of totally going off their HIV medications while they struggle to get their meth use under control.

Reback, Larkins, and Shoptaw[7] interviewed twenty-three gay and bisexual men living with HIV who were participating in an outpatient drug treatment research project on methamphetamine abuse, all of whom acknowledged that their drug use interfered with their adherence to antiretroviral medication. Unplanned nonadherence was associated with meth-related disruptions in eating and sleeping, while *planned* nonadherence was identified as a strategy in recognition that a rigorous medication schedule would not be maintained while using methamphetamine.

Another group of men reported that nonadherence was related to their participation in sexual activities or to concerns about mixing methamphetamine and medications. The authors found that, "even though the men did not take their medications according to prescribed directions, they did not interpret skipping, stretching, or modifying their medication doses as non-adherence." The authors found that these medication adjustments were viewed as a positive coping strategy that served to create a sense of control over their lives.

Short-term drug and sex-related non-adherence was rationalized as an *acceptable compromise*. The men did not consider their partial or inconsistent adherence as anything other than full adherence. They believed that if they caught up with missed doses by increasing their dosage for two or three days following a drug and sex-related interruption, they would still qualify as *medication adherent*.

The inability of many HIV-infected individuals to adhere to their medication regime makes abstinence from meth the most viable option. Once free of recreational drugs, the responses to antiretroviral therapy by former methamphetamine dependent persons are similar to those of non-substance abusing control subjects.[8]

The combination of methamphetamine and antiviral medications is deleterious as well, both in terms of antiretroviral adherence and the potential for a drug overdose. Methamphetamine can interact with HIV medications, particularly protease inhibitors, resulting in increased toxicity or death.[9] Halkitis, Parsons, and Stirrat[10] also found that the effect of methamphetamine has been demonstrated to be two or three times greater for individuals on combination therapy, especially combinations including ritonavir (Norvir).

One physician who specializes in the treatment of HIV among gay men reported that many of the HIV deaths he sees are related to methamphetamine. Men taking meth not only miss their HIV meds, but they miss other medications as well. He reported morbidity related to treatable infections that got out of control because the meth users did not take their antibiotics as prescribed. He also reported general neglect of self-care. One man, who like many other users had lost a significant amount of weight and who was suffering from untreated anal warts, stated that despite his physical condition he could not resist compulsively seeking sex on a daily basis. He reported signing onto Manhunt, an online sex site for gay men, and hooking up with other men. The physician was incredulous that anyone would want to have sex with his patient, and yet finding sex partners was not a problem. He was able to find other men as hungry for compulsive meth-sex as he was. He stated his sex partners would, "go around the warts," if they were contacting his anal area with their hands, mouths, or genitalia.

Methamphetamine may also have an impact on transmission of HIV in ways that are beyond the obvious. Methamphetamine appears to affect how the body fights the virus itself, which has tremendous implications for the deadly synergy of HIV and meth. Urbina and Jones[11] note that HIV may have an immunomodulatory (capable of modifying or altering one or more immune system activity) effect, particularly by impairing CD8 lymphocyte function. Simply stated, methamphetamine seems to impair the ability of the immune system to fight HIV following exposure, thus facilitating the establishment of infection.

The Other HIV Cocktail

Several reports suggest that expanding recreational use of sildenafil (Viagra) in conjunction with methamphetamine is contributing to increases in the rates of HIV, syphilis, and other sexually transmitted diseases in the US. In a study involving 388 MSM,[12] 16 percent reported using methamphetamine and 6 percent reported using sildenafil during their most recent episode of anal intercourse. Meth users were twice as likely as nonusers to have engaged in condomless receptive anal intercourse and sildenafil users were 6.5 times more likely to report having had condomless, insertive anal intercourse. Sildenafil use did not, however, appear to increase condomless receptive anal intercourse.

Wong[13] reported that MSM who used methamphetamine and sildenafil in combination were over six times more likely to be diagnosed with syphilis than those who abstained from these drugs. In another study involving 1,263 MSM seeking clinic services for sexually transmitted diseases,[14] 17.4 percent reported using methamphetamine during the four preceding weeks. When compared to nonusers, those who used meth were more than two times as likely to be living with HIV, 4.9 times as likely to be diagnosed with syphilis, and 1.7 times as likely to be diagnosed with gonorrhea.

The seductive power of methamphetamine provides a near perfect fit with the contours of the sexual desire of gay men, first binding to them with relentless force, and then distorting them to the point that many men begin not to recognize themselves or their partners. To better understand this phenomenon it is necessary to venture into the inner sexual landscape and explore sexual scripts, templates, and the erotic potential of fantasies, taboo, and power. Part II is your guide to this universe.

▪ PART II

EXPLORING THE SEXUAL UNIVERSE

5

Sexual Templates, Themes, and Shadows

Everyone, gay or straight, male or female, spends a considerable portion of their lives with sex on their mind. Humans are born with a basic sexual energy that, over time, is molded by a variety of forces into our erotic identity. Some of our earliest memories involve attraction to significant persons in our lives, which grows into childhood play, and blossoms during adolescence into a sexual life that extends over the arc of our lifespans to old age.

> **On meth I became a bigger freak, a fetishist, however you want to put it. I found sex without meth simply uninteresting.**
>
> — METH USER

Although sex has been the focus of a significant amount of scholarly research, sexual desire has confounded academics and the public alike for many years because it cannot be easily quantified. Early on, Freud proposed that our libido conflicts with the conventions of civilized society, resulting in neuroses to which nearly every adult was doomed. Despite theoretical limitations based on the attitudes of a different era, sexual conflict and tension continue to provide a foundation for understanding the sexual landscape.

Sex in our culture, and especially sex falling outside the traditional boundaries of "normal," is at once pervasive, yet shrouded in mystery and misunderstanding. Our society has an overabundance of sexual images but also a simultaneous lack of deeper sexual understanding.

We are bombarded with advertising images using sex to capture our attention to sell products or services, however, while sex is everywhere, people are often reluctant or embarrassed to talk about it directly. I have seen many gay men in my office who have had sexual contact with literally thousands of other men, but who have a remarkable lack of knowledge about many sexual concerns, including safer sex and skills related to intimacy. Sexual quantity does not necessarily translate effectively into sexual quality or self-knowledge.

The purpose of the chapters in Part II is to demystify, to the extent possible in this context, individual sexual desire and each person's uniqueness. Then, the impact of meth and other compulsive behaviors on each man's sexuality will be explored. For many years, sexology, the study of human sexuality, focused on the mechanics of sex while the psychological elements of desire remained much less understood than their physiological counterparts. Any deviation from heterosexual penis-vaginal intercourse was labeled a sexual perversion and was believed to result from various neuroses.

In the socially conservative post-World War II era, entomologist and zoologist Alfred Kinsey turned his attention to human sexuality and published significant sexual research[1,2] that was, by nature of the times, written in a dense, clinical language. For the first time he quantified an estimate of homosexuality in society with his well-known Kinsey Scale, stating that about 10 percent of men in the United States had experienced orgasms in sexual intercourse with other men.

Kinsey downplayed erotic themes in favor of orgasm, a physiological response that was far easier to measure. Thus, the defining feature of much of Alfred Kinsey's well-known sexual behavior research was orgasm itself. This "know it when you see it" approach thereby focused only on the sexual cycle, totally ignoring elements of sexual desire.

In the 1960s, the famed husband and wife sex researchers Masters and Johnson wrote about the human sexual response[3,4] and worked with couples to increase their sexual functioning through a series of homework assignments such as sensate focus, a physical communication exercise. Their belief was that if inhibitions were reduced and "mechanical" problems of a couple's interaction were resolved, good sex would result. While still a valuable framework and exercise, this approach ignored issues central to the necessary first stage in the sexual cycle: desire itself.

Scholars have recently begun to examine sexual desire in more comprehensive ways. Some of this work, such as that of Robert Stoller,[5] is an updated descendant of Freud's psychoanalytic model, which has been further developed in fascinating work by scholars such as Michael Bader[6] and Jack Morin. These approaches view sex as a fragile balance between simultaneously caring for and pleasing our partner, and being selfish and using them for our own sexual gratification, a theme which, as has already been noted, is only amplified by methamphetamine. Ironically, elements that amplify sexual desire also have the potential to inhibit it. For example, strong emotions such as anger, shame, guilt, and fear can either arouse or dampen sexual desire. Other examples of this paradox relevant to methamphetamine include the mental and emotional juggling involved in the thrill of breaking taboos, the racing fear of being discovered in a sexual act, or drug-induced liberation from the shackles of sexual shame.

Sexual Templates

One issue central to a book about gay men, sex, and methamphetamine is sexual orientation itself. While the issue of choice regarding sexual orientation is sometimes still mentioned, there is a broad consensus among scholars that sexual orientation is not a personal choice (although expression of it is) but rather the result of a complex process largely rooted in biology.

The other various physical, emotional, and intellectual characteristics of someone that we find sexually attractive are described as a sexual template. Elements include features such as height, race, hair color, build, and temperament. Researchers such as John Money[7,8] and William Granzig have made significant contributions to our understanding of sexual templates. This understanding of templates makes clear how a drug such as methamphetamine hijacks our brains and distorts our deepest fantasies into unrecognizable drives with supercharged and destructive erotic power.

These sexual templates set into play lifelong patterns of attraction and arousal that are both conscious and unconscious. Some people rigidly adhere to their templates while others are more flexible in choosing sexual partners. Very tall or very short individuals could be part of someone's template. One person might be very rigid (meaning they are *only* attracted to persons of a specific height) while someone else might be more flexible in that characteristic (meaning that height isn't as important as, say, eye color or temperament). Age is another characteristic of sexual templates that is easy to identify. Most persons find themselves attracted to someone plus or minus five to ten years of their own age. As they get older, the objects of their attraction age as well. I have had clients, however, who as young men themselves were attracted to their peers. As they aged, however, their attraction remained rigidly fixed on men much younger than themselves, often resulting in social and intimate partner complications.

Money coined the term "lovemap,"[9] referring to the sexual template in the mind that depicts one's idealized lover and the erotic activities, whether fantasy or actual sexual behavior, that one finds most stimulating. Money felt that templates develop at an early age, and perhaps even prenatally, beginning with hormonal washes of the brain that result in either heterosexual or homosexual erotic attraction and further evolving through normal sexual play among children. Such behavior at a young age, while typically discouraged in our society, is common to all primates.

While most of us make it through the perils of growing up, for some people things can go very wrong. According to Money, a child's template can be "vandalized," either by well-meaning adults or through deprivation, neglect, prohibition, or abuse. Templates are most vulnerable between the ages of five and eight, when sexual traumas more significantly disrupt their consolidation. Money proposes that these templates are extremely resistant to change following puberty and contain specific details of an individual's ideal sexual partner that last a lifetime, including attraction regarding body type, race, color, and temperament.

What types of vandalism occur? Activities such as corporal punishment can result in "panic erections" and lead to lifelong patterns of arousal linked with punishment. The eroticization of punishment and even violence is best explained when a powerful aversion or attraction to a particular experience undergoes a reversal, as in pain to pleasure, tragedy to triumph, or terror into euphoria. According to Money, any vandalism of a template will result in a paraphilia, that is, the eroticizing of non-traditional objects or behaviors. For unknown reasons, paraphilias are much more common among men. Examples include gerontophilia (erotic interest in elderly people), masochism (erotic attraction to suffering, being bound, or otherwise humiliated), and sexual fetishism (erotic interest in non-living objects such as leather or shoes). While no specific classification exists, there are dozens of paraphilias that include arousal derived from a variety of inanimate objects or situations. Some sexologists view paraphilias as a "heroic effort" by the subconscious to rescue lust from total elimination in the template. In other words, although a child may learn that it is not safe to express sexual feelings toward other persons, the subconscious, needing a sexual outlet, creates an avenue to express erotic energy toward "safe" inanimate objects or non-traditional behaviors such as high-heeled shoes, underclothing, or a non-genital body part such as the foot. An unfortunate effect of this process, however, is the separation of lust and love (or sexual behavior from emotional attachment).

It is impossible to fully trace the development of any individual's template. Sometimes the elements of specific incidents can be identified, but more typically their origins remain elusive. One client, Stanley, found himself powerfully drawn to both muscular men and voyeurism. His case illustrates the incorporation of several paraphilic themes into his template.

Stanley grew up in a rural area, the son of an academic and the youngest of four brothers. His parents were both extremely uncomfortable with displays of affection, and Stanley reported always feeling uncertain about being able to give or receive love. This emotional insecurity was compounded by his stature. He was physically small and was frequently bullied in school. Consequently, he was always more comfortable among adults and rarely identified with peers on a social level. At an early age Stanley began watching wrestling on television and looking at muscle magazines. While viewing these strong men Stanley fantasized that he had their power. Years later, when he experienced puberty, Stanley found himself having erections while watching these men.

When he came for therapy as an adult, Stanley's sexual template still retained a strong attraction to muscular, male bodies, as well as a preference for sexual arousal through voyeurism (known technically as scoptophilia). Once an element is incorporated into a sexual template it is nearly impossible to alter. For that reason, it was not worthwhile to spend time in therapy trying to eradicate these elements of Stanley's template, in just the same way that aversion therapy (trying to change behavior by exposing someone simultaneously to the stimuli and to discomfort) or corrective homosexual therapies (to "cure" same-sex orientation) are pointless and actually harmful. Instead, we focused on self-regulation techniques for any nonconsensual voyeurism and more self-acceptance of the body types he found attractive. Because sexual templates can be expanded to include other elements, we also explored new characteristics or behaviors that held erotic interest for Stanley.

Sexual Templates and Meth

Once templates develop they are, then, extremely resistant to change. Whatever ignites a person's erotic fire as an adolescent will largely be what stokes them as an adult. It is possible, with much effort, to deny or refuse to act upon one's template. For example, sexual attraction to other men, if that is part of one's template, is lifelong and unchanging. Some choose not to act upon these desires because of negative social pressure. Indeed, expressing them (or not) is the only element of choice concerning homosexuality. Sexual orientation will remain consistent even if not acted upon or even consciously acknowledged.

Of course, homosexuality is no longer deemed deviant, but the permanency of a template's features is seen in other elements deemed taboo as well. An erotic attraction to a pre-pubescent body is, while socially taboo, persistent. Someone experiencing this attraction might cope by expanding their sexual template to include other more appropriate behaviors, but such erotic attraction cannot simply be unlearned. It persists, like other characteristics, in the sexual template. Consequently, an adult may be able to resist acting out on an ephebephilic fantasy, but he will not be able to eliminate it from his template.

When methamphetamine is ingested and used for sexual enhancement, several different processes are cast into motion. First, meth's disinhibiting properties expose elements of sexual templates that may have previously been beyond conscious reach. Meth breaks down the barriers between what is conscious and what has been repressed. One's sexual template could be viewed as a large, ancient stone carving buried in shifting sands. On it are inscribed dozens of features of ideal sexual partners and behaviors. Some of these features may be familiar—they are exposed to the light and consciously known. Others, however, have long been buried beneath the surface. By disinhibiting one's ability to keep these features hidden, meth, in effect, creates a powerful wind that scatters away the sand and exposes long-secret elements of the sexual template.

Many men using meth have shocked themselves with sexual fantasies or behaviors, most of which, unlike the blackout experience of alcohol, are fully recalled once the effects of the meth have diminished. These newly revealed (or created) sexual attractions are disturbing and even traumatic, but they have likely been a part of an individual's template his entire life. This results in the unsettling experience of discovering a "stranger" within, and a side of oneself for which there can be a great deal of disdain.

Meth impacts templates in a second way: permeability. Each of us has our own unique level of rigidity concerning adherence to the elements of our sexual template. People typically remain attracted to others who are of a similar age, even as they get older. For example, one client named Mike recalled being attracted to a twenty-eight year old when he was thirty, and now at age fifty-five he finds men in their fifties appealing. In other words, the age of people he finds attractive has consistently changed as he aged. Another client named Bob, however, is attracted only to men who are between twenty-one and twenty-five years of age. This was the case when he was twenty-one and has remained so as he aged. His template is more rigid than Mike's. Someone else might prefer Hispanics, but easily be attracted to other ethnicities, while a different person might be totally turned off by Hispanics. There are infinite combinations in the specifics that comprise our templates.

Meth affects this permeability. Whatever level of rigid adherence to the template was experienced before meth, it will be broken while on the drug. This drug, in effect, blasts apart the sexual template so that it no longer contains elements bound together in a cohesive way. Erotic fantasies spill like flooding waters into dark caverns, sweeping the user along on an intense and sometimes terrifying sexual adventure. Many men using meth discover that their preferred sexual "type" or behavior is no longer relevant. As one man said, "any warm hole will suffice." Concern for sexual and moral choices vanishes as one's primary purpose becomes simply experiencing the next erotic sensation.

In summary, methamphetamine alters the sexual template in two ways. First, it uncovers elements that our conscious mind has kept secret even from ourselves and that may be extremely unsettling. Second, meth snaps the tethers that hold behavior and fantasy to one's template, thereby releasing a compressed erotic energy that flies in many directions and sexualizes all sorts of behaviors, resulting in short-term pleasure and long-term harm.

Sexual Scripts

The notion of sexual scripts grew out of a need to understand the psychological or socially constructed elements of sexual desire, which the groundbreaking Kinsey studies had avoided. Two researchers at the Kinsey Institute, John Gagnon and William Simon, ultimately brought together the idea of sexual behavior and self-concept in the groundbreaking book *Sexual Conduct.*[10] They wrote that human sexualities are socially produced, organized, maintained, and transformed in complex ways, and that categories such as "homosexual" or "heterosexual" are vastly over-simplistic.

Gagnon and Simon proposed three sets of scripts that define our sexual behavior. The first set of these is cultural scripts, which flow from the customs and traditions around us and result in expectations about appropriate and inappropriate sexual behavior. Cultural scripts are not chosen but rather imparted to us. Even rebellious sexual activity, such as transgressive behavior that flaunts taboos, can be viewed within the larger framework of a cultural sexual script. The second set, called interpersonal scripts, is more personal and grows from the interaction of our personality with family, peers, and other significant individuals. The third set of scripts is called intrapsychic (or within the mind) scripts, which allow us to develop images about our actual and ideal sexual selves, fantasies, and expectations. As Morin notes,[11] these are expressions of each person's unique response to his or her life experiences, beginning as a young child. Consequently, there are an infinite variety of these scripts reflecting the "eccentricities of each individual's erotic mind."[12]

This third type, intrapsychic erotic scripts, is fascinating because these scripts often elude conscious awareness. One of the frightening aspects of methamphetamine is that it brings some of these elements into consciousness. Meth also reduces inhibitions about sharing aspects of these scripts, resulting in feelings of shame as elements are revealed "under the influence." Many times individuals keep their erotic scripts to themselves, not even sharing them with their most trusted and intimate partners.

Sexual scripts often have themes that remain simple and consistent, even while the elements and characters of a script vary tremendously. People often have a "Core Erotic Theme," which is the central story line in their sexual fantasy that is utilized repeatedly to achieve sexual stimulation and ultimately orgasm. Our "fantasy self" and "fantasy sex partners" can be cloaked in a variety of costumes, body types, emotions, and geographic settings, but the essential emotional and sexual dynamics are remarkably consistent. Under the influence of drugs, porn, or other addictive behaviors, these sexual scripts become highly focused and deeply grooved in the mind. Over time they become the only means by which a person can reach orgasm, resulting in sexual dysfunction.

As noted, meth also influences sexual scripts by eroticizing taboo elements. Such darker features produce shame and self-judgment because they contain *fantasy* behaviors that are non-conforming and self-destructive, and are inconsistent with an individual's sense of self. For example, meth use may promote extended drug-sex sessions of consenting adults in which a group "pounds," "wrecks," or otherwise defiles the "hole" of a willing bottom. In other cases various forms of aggressive (and dangerous) sexual behavior is enabled with the use of meth and other drugs.

Erotic themes can also be viewed as a desire for wholeness and completion. Tripp[13] observed their effect on sexual attraction when we select partners who value our strengths and compensate for our weaknesses. Tripp proposed the concept of "exporting," that is, receiving validation and boosting our self-esteem, when we are valued by another and "importing," finding characteristics in another that fill in missing aspects of ourselves.

The core erotic theme of one client, Matthew, illustrates how multiple scripts have a central theme. Matthew was a successful thirty-eight year old gay white male who was building his own law practice. Although initially seeking help for his methamphetamine dependence, Matthew ultimately realized that his troubling sexual behavior on meth was rooted in his core erotic script, which developed long before he encountered drugs. This theme involved the seduction of powerful, dangerous men. The essential core of this script was that Matthew used his fantasy sexual power to seduce them, containing the risk and becoming their ally. This was only arousing if he consciously maintained an awareness of fear throughout the fantasy. This fear, simultaneously combined with the emotional safety of fantasy-bonding with a powerful man, served as an aphrodisiac that ultimately powered his orgasm.

While this theme remained constant, it was expressed through a variety of individual scripts that varied based on the identity of the dangerous leading man. He cited a fantasy cast of mafia kingpins, Colombian drug lords, mercenaries, gang leaders, even men from other times and places that could, as long as they fit the central theme, be plugged in and push him into sexual overdrive.

For most of his life, Matthew's colorful cast of characters had not caused him any significant emotional distress. Under the influence of meth, however, Matthew began to realize that his scripts were evolving into more disturbing patterns that were increasingly what therapists call ego-dystonic, or inconsistent with his fundamental values and personality. His fantasy scripts began to involve a wider range of violence in which Matthew was not only a witness, but ultimately became a participant. Aggression became prominent and vivid. Acts of brutality became central to the script, and Matthew found himself, under the influence of meth, becoming erotically aroused by these scenarios. Matthew had begun "importing" power from his sex partner in a quest for wholeness to supplant his own feelings of powerlessness. In other words, he reclaimed a lost sense of empowerment by affiliating—even under dangerous scenarios—with powerful men.

Meth distorted the elements of his erotic theme, upsetting the balance of empathy and objectification in his fantasy. Meth allowed Matthew to rage with fantasy power, and the degree to which Matthew felt powerless was the extent to which he embraced and abused that power in his meth-driven fantasies. Matthew had developed a new shadow theme, and with it, a sexual problem.

Shadow Themes

Shadow themes are a normal part of healthy sexuality and develop naturally as we distance ourselves from thoughts and feelings that might lead to disapproval or abandonment by those whose assistance we need to survive. Carl Jung used the term "shadow" to describe anything within us that is unconscious, repressed, undeveloped, and denied. He noted that confrontation of our own shadows is necessary for self-awareness and growth. Likewise, acquainting ourselves with and understanding our shadow themes are necessary steps toward sexual fulfillment and self-acceptance.

Although shadow fantasies consist of disturbing themes, they rarely cause harm. The vast majority of people have no desire to act out these fantasies in real life, yet play out these erotic scenarios either in their head or in carefully controlled settings complete with props. Learning more about our shadows can, as Jung noted, help us reintegrate rejected aspects of ourselves that they represent. Knowledge of our shadows empowers us with understanding and increased choice in all areas of our lives.

While unacknowledged psychological shadows often result in self-destructive behavior, those that arise as a result of drugs at work in the brain create even more harm. Matthew's ingestion of methamphetamine distorted his fantasies in a way that was ultimately destructive not only for his sense of self, but also for his sexual functioning. He came away from the experience drawn toward the heightened sexual sensations on meth, yet ultimately traumatized by the graphic sexual images and sensations that flowed out of his own mind after months of drug use.

He also discovered that sexual scripts and their shadow themes are more or less permanent once formed. Elements that become embedded in one's template can rarely be expunged. When Matthew tried to back away from the seduction of his dark sexual scripts, he found that he could not become aroused. The heightened sexual sensations on methamphetamine had become fused with his fantasies, and when he tried to banish one, so went the other.

Sexual recovery includes not only breaking the bond between the meth and sexual arousal, but becoming familiar with one's sexual scripts as well. While elements of a sexual script are largely permanent, it is also true that they are constantly evolving and changing in response to our thoughts and feelings. While we cannot eliminate portions of our template, we can add new features to it. Matthew likened his healing journey of redifferentiating sex from drug use to the wall of a dark room on which was engraved his sexual template. Methamphetamine had illuminated one small corner with a light so bright that he felt there was nothing else on the wall. But when he extinguished the meth "light" and allowed his eyes to readjust, a complex mosaic of other sexually desirable features was revealed, some familiar and some newly discovered, toward which he could direct his erotic energies. By avoiding the drug-related erotic features and favoring healthier ones, he gradually began to rewire his erotic drives.

The Impact of Shame

Many individuals, and especially gay men, experience high levels of shame, the depths of which affect their erotic lives in ways that remain elusive to conscious recognition. Shame results from verbal, physical, emotional, and/or sexual abuse. Children are dependent on their caregivers for survival and will protect that relationship, even if it means creating negative self-beliefs. Children have no other emotional option except to blame themselves for abuse by their caregiver and to believe that they have somehow caused this unconscionable behavior. They will take responsibility for abuse and for the reactions of others that, over time, become fixed in the form of core beliefs that operate below the conscious surface but that affect all aspects of our relationships, including erotic themes. Part III contains more information on healing shame.

Shame is built on false core beliefs about ourselves that are taught to us. Core beliefs are best described[14] as key convictions that we maintain about ourselves. They include thoughts about the kind of person we are or will become, our place within our family and the world at large, and how we expect others to respond to us. They can be conscious or lie buried in the subconscious. Every child struggles with some negative feedback from the world, but if that child maintains a sense of self-worth, most damaging effects can be mitigated. If those small kernels of self-worth are squelched, however, a child begins to incorporate what Morin[15] calls an "unconscious legacy" in which, at some level, he begins to think he deserves to be treated badly. If these persist, sexual excitement and self-hate can fuse. Early experiences of self-devaluation become linked with arousal.

Should that happen, erotic scripts begin to take on dark scenarios that, while momentarily exciting, are ultimately disturbing. Their purpose is to find an indirect route to self-affirmation by constructing fantasies that are demeaning to self or to someone else in a form of repetition and reversal. For example, someone from whom power has been taken can recreate a scenario in which he/she simultaneously surrenders power but maintains the ability to say "no" and regulate the amount of helplessness. Or, someone who has felt abused or demeaned can regain control through scenarios that involve demeaning others. While these "workarounds" allow sexual release, they do not serve to heal those old emotional wounds, but to actually maintain them.

Methamphetamine is akin to gasoline thrown onto the fire of erotic scripts. It distorts erotic fantasies to the point where they are unrecognizable. They no longer serve as the carefully constructed scenarios that perfectly adjust our core beliefs to compensate for unbridled erotic expression during sexual encounters. Sexual fantasies on meth become contorted and twisted and, while under the influence of the drug, generate tremendous erotic appeal with little enduring satisfaction. They ultimately "overwrite" existing scripts so that when the drug is withdrawn, an individual's pathway to erotic release is lost or disconnected. The same process is true for any state-dependent sexuality, such as that created by cocaine, pornography, or other mood-changing behaviors or processes. Once this occurs, there can be a total loss of erotic drive if the mood-altering behavior ceases. For most men who are first trying to remain clean from meth, the only fantasies that create arousal are those that involve the drug, and they often lead directly to cravings.

Erotic Crisis

Loss of erotic desire represents a crisis that is a profound problem for anyone who has experienced the fusion of methamphetamine (or, as noted above, any other drug or mood-altering behavior) with sex. A parallel phenomenon is seen in individuals who, through personal growth, begin to improve their self-esteem and reduce shame. They also experience a growing incompatibility with their now outdated erotic scripts, which originally evolved to compensate for negative core beliefs. When significant emotional growth occurs, the sexual script is no longer needed to make up for low self-esteem or the feeling that he or she is an unworthy outsider. The individual is left feeling better about himself, but unable to become aroused in the old, familiar ways. Emotional growth can even be sabotaged by old scripts that are resistant to change and act as a drag on an individual's development.

Morin suggests[16] that a healing question to ask oneself is, "What turns me on when I am feeling strong?" This question could easily be modified to be, "What turns me on when I am not high?" For many men just off meth, the first answer to this question is an emphatic, "Nothing turns me on when I'm not high." Asking this question, however, is an excellent way to begin to examine elements of sexual scripts that have long been overshadowed by the excesses of the drug. Many central themes of our erotic scripts (for example, the thrill of surrendering control) remain consistent over the lifespan. Creative use of fantasy helps us rediscover people, settings, and behaviors that are unassociated with drugs yet still stimulate and energize our sexuality.

Finally, the spiritual component of sex should be noted. It is another major piece of the erotic spectrum that is set adrift under the influence of methamphetamine. While the intensity of meth-sex can be so heightened that some might describe it as "spiritual," most would agree that meth causes an internalized focus on one's own sensual experience that overrides many layers of a strong and profound energetic connection between two persons. An authentic intimate bond between two people creates a satisfying feeling of wholeness and connection that results from the harmony not just of an erotic script brought to life, but of a present emotional, physical, and spiritual connection. In such cases, lust and love overlap. Meth, in fact, disconnects lust and love.

Thus far, we have examined sexual scripts, templates, and shadow themes, along with the central role of core beliefs, especially shame. In the second part of our insider's guide to the sexual universe, we go deeper into the very nature of sexual desire.

6

The Aphrodisiac Effect of Secret Desires

Joseph, a white, gay male in his mid-forties, has a successful career as a travel agent, running his own business. In the last ten years, he has had several periods of intense substance abuse, most recently involving methamphetamine. Six years ago he began using meth recreationally to increase his sexual sensations and ultimately found his way into recovery, which he maintained for another three years. Family stressors reignited a desire to numb feelings, and he relapsed on meth, this time losing his business and ending up in long-term, residential treatment. While there, he began a sexual relationship with another client, a heterosexual black male named William, who allowed Joseph to fellate him in exchange for cash. This continued after both were released from the program, when William returned to his girlfriend and Joseph tried to rebuild his life.

> Meth allowed me to live out my darkest fantasies… and destroyed anything I valued.
>
> — METH USER

Joseph remained obsessed with William and would frequently call and text him until William responded and allowed Joseph to perform sex on him for cash, usually accompanied by demeaning language. While Joseph found the experience humiliating, it only heightened his arousal. Joseph ultimately became so distraught by his obsession that he relapsed again on meth, this time slamming (injecting). He was fortunate to get back into recovery quickly, although he totally lost his livelihood and now faced additional drug charges.

The more unobtainable the person, the more heightened was Joseph's sexual desire for them. Although he realized the situation with William was destructive, he seemed incapable of ignoring the force that irrationally escalated his desire and pulled him into verbally abusive sexual encounters with William. Joseph was experiencing what Jack Morin[1] describes as one of four "cornerstones" of eroticism that give life to one's sexual templates. These are the interpersonal dynamics that, once incorporated into a sexual template, ratchet up the level of desire. They are universal—not unique to gay men or to substance abusers—and while each cornerstone is not evident in every sexual fantasy, at least one, and often several, can usually be identified in the details of an individual's sexual patterns. All of these cornerstones derive from the dance between attraction and obstacles. They are longing and anticipation, breaking taboos, searching for power, and overcoming ambivalence.

Longing and Anticipation

The first cornerstone Morin describes is "longing and anticipation," which, simply stated, is the notion that sexual arousal is heightened when someone is unobtainable (longing), or not yet but may soon be available (anticipation). The challenge of overcoming this "unobtainability" increases sexual desire. This is a theme that emerges in childhood with parental attractions (the unattainable loved one) and is expressed in fairytales such as Cinderella. It continues through school, when many students fantasize about a teacher, and it thrives in adulthood. Perhaps predictably, elimination or reduction of longing and anticipation frequently cools the sexual heat. Nearly everyone knows a couple who survived a long-distance relationship only to have it crumble when they finally succeeded in living together.

In therapy Joseph was ultimately able to understand that the overpowering desire he felt for William was, in part, fueled by the impossibility of this attraction. This was not primarily a matter of race or even social standing, although these played a role in further distancing William. Joseph knew that William, a heterosexual male totally dismissive of him, could *never* be obtained, which heightened his desire even more. The situation ultimately erupted when William came to Joseph's house for sex and, after Joseph fell asleep, robbed him. Even that incident couldn't totally dampen Joseph's desire for William. When Joseph thought about other men in his life for whom he felt this charged desire, he discovered that they had all been unobtainable, both physically and emotionally.

For Joseph this discovery was a revelation. Looking back over his life he was able to identify many men who had expressed desire for him and were willing and available, but Joseph, deeming them uninteresting and undesirable, quickly dismissed them. Ultimately Joseph was able to begin working on issues of self-worth, and relied less on hopeless longing and anticipation to fuel his sexual desire.

Breaking Taboos

Morin's second cornerstone is violating prohibitions. The widely-recognized appeal of breaking taboos has long been a staple of gay sexual life. Maintaining the fine balance between inhibition and titillation fuels sexual heat. Because of such strong societal disapproval about homosexuality, a central issue in the coming out process involves finding the esteem within oneself to honor one's inner feelings, despite emotional, social, and sometimes physical sanctions. Even after breaking these barriers and "coming out," most gay men carry vestiges of internalized homophobia, whereby a variety of sexual behaviors, thoughts, and fantasies become charged with shame. Shame inhibits sexual expression, but paradoxically, sometimes the thought, and eventually the act, of transgressing the taboo by indulging in the behavior becomes highly erotic and serves as a potent aphrodisiac.

In 1973, Andrew Tobias published his memoir *The Best Little Boy in the World*, in which he posited that many young gay males, in the face of stigma from family and society, bolster their sense of worthiness by striving for perfection through overachievement. This sets a course in which some behaviors, especially sexual, that do not fit into a carefully constructed and socially desirable persona, are driven underground. Many gay men identify with being "the best little boy in the world," and some thrive on "being bad," at least sexually. As Morin states,[2] "without boundaries to push against, there is no joy in naughtiness." Like other erotic elements, maintaining an awareness that one is violating a boundary keeps its erotic power alive. As the degree of taboo diminishes, so does the erotic appeal of the behavior.

This desire to act as a sexual outlaw is fueled by methamphetamine. The drug reduces inhibition and turns feelings about the taboo behavior inside out, meaning that what once was shameful and secret is, on meth, titillating. The drug drives these feelings to such a degree that it quickly moves men through a phase of healthy affirmation and self-assertion into flaunting of sexual taboos and disregarding the health of themselves and their sexual partners. Many meth users I know describe a phase of their drug use when meth took away any sexual self-doubt, making them feel proud to act out their lust in any way they could. Such persistent use, however, inevitably results in destruction of sexual satisfaction and self-concept.

Gay men, having been harshly judged by religion, society, and even their own families, sometimes reject sexual boundaries altogether and feel entitled to unbridled sexual expression. Through the act of coming out, which is ultimately an act of self-love, many gay men reject the hurtful judgments of others (although many self-critical beliefs are internalized and remain hidden) and the sexual limits that have been imposed. Coming out is taken by some as license to act out sexually; behavioral parameters are rejected.

Despite overt transgressive behaviors, what often remains below the surface is the internalized belief that something inside is amiss. This tension between an "anything goes" approach to sex and internal core beliefs provides both elements, attraction, and obstacle, each of which is supercharged by methamphetamine.

Meth creates yet another paradox with regard to taboo. Before using the drug, many men find that a small element of taboo behavior is adequate to fuel the equation and result in excitement. Because meth disinhibits, however, many old behaviors and fantasies that were once taboo enough to result in excitement become less powerful. A meth user often feels so disinhibited that longstanding "taboo fantasy favorites," whether being tied up with rope or having sex in a public place, will no longer balance the equation and result in excitement.

More extreme taboo behavior is needed: riskier, rougher, darker sex. Clients report escalations in behavior such as being injected with meth by a stranger, acting out a fantasy rape scene, or any other scenario they think will ignite an erotic spark.

Tommy never thought he would end up like this. He laughingly described himself as a nice kid from Kansas, "just like Dorothy," who was basically clueless when he moved to San Francisco to discover himself and fulfill his desire to live freely as a gay man. He soon encountered sex and all kinds of drugs, including methamphetamine. He found the high from smoking tina really enhanced sex for him, at least at first.

One night while partying with several men, he was introduced to injecting meth. Tommy felt at once terrified and thrilled, and proceeded to let a stranger shoot him up. Some taboo barrier had been crossed, and there was no turning back. He began to inject whenever he used meth and soon felt very competent at injecting himself or others.

More disturbing was Tommy's increasing fascination with needles and injecting. He would sometimes play with the needles without the drug, and when he had blood drawn at his physician's office he was powerfully triggered to use meth. Given his upbringing, there was something about injecting drugs that was so rebellious that he found it tremendously appealing. He began to hang out only with other men who injected, taking pride in identifying as a "slammer."

Tommy described another strange but related obsession. He found himself spending hours watching other men inject themselves online. He discovered video chat rooms devoted to slamming, and realized that other men were as addicted to the process of injecting as they were to their drugs.

The power of taboo and violating prohibitions is clearly expressed with the thrill of injection drug use and the desire to self-identify as a "slammer." Much of the arousing power derives from the fact that the behavior itself is considered taboo.[3] This nice kid from Kansas suddenly saw himself as an outlaw of sorts, and he found that thrilling. The same phenomenon is true of another taboo behavior, barebacking. In just the same way, men who bareback tend to congregate together, gravitate toward certain websites, and identify with the terminology and its explicit "in-your-face" connotation.

How far can it go? Is there an end to the pursuit of breaking taboos? Many men are physically harmed by acquiring a disease such as HIV, hepatitis, or a variety of other life-threatening problems resulting directly from the chemical effects of the drug. Many more get hurt emotionally, feeling shameful, hopeless, and depressed as their bodies give out and they are no longer able to achieve that sexual intensity that once came so easily with meth. Eventually they watch their sexual fantasies careen out of sight like a runaway train while they are left behind on the track, feeling sick and empty and frustrated that they can't capture that unnatural sexual high again, and finding it nearly impossible to return back to what was once "normal sex."

Searching for Power

The third cornerstone of eroticism involves the search for power, which, at its most blatant, involves ritualized acting out of dominance and submission. It also exists with infinite variety in the form of subtle negotiations and exchanges. There are two sexual strategies whereby people overcome feelings of powerlessness.[4] The first is through direct action, such as taking steps to assert one's will. The second is what Morin calls "highly refined surrendering," in which submission in a safe and scripted setting allows someone to regain a sense of control. Patterns related to interpersonal power are learned early in childhood and acquire erotic overtones as we age. Consequently, for many, themes of taking or surrendering power are a central part of their erotic scripts.

Many gay men utilize the labels of "bottom" or "top" to describe their core erotic attraction. Whether a gay man is exclusively one or the other, or if there is a continuum of preferences and behaviors that are consistent or situational, or if a dichotomous construct is even relevant, remains debated. Nor do concepts like "top" and "bottom" match physical description. One client who was a competitive bodybuilder was continually frustrated by men who wanted him to be the "top," and to whom he had to explain that *his* erotic script called for him to be the receptive sexual partner.

What is clear is that, whether top, bottom, dominant, or submissive, both parties, when engaging in reciprocal sex involving power exchange, gain a sense of control and affirmation through their respective, chosen roles. A submissive gains power by surrendering it by choice and in a scripted manner. A dominant gives power by investing erotic energy and skill in the needs of the submissive.

The attraction lies in the erotic drive attached to a person's relationship with power. For example, is someone surrendering power, defiant of power, or taking or displaying power? As has been mentioned earlier, sexual fantasies serve to create an emotional safety zone for sex where issues of control or worry or other negative thoughts and feelings can be neutralized. It is not uncommon for someone with a history of abuse to recreate scenes where power is again surrendered, but this time in a highly controlled and thus personally empowering way.

The obstacles in these scenarios tend to be the emotions attached to the power relationship. For example, a sense of danger dramatically heightens the act of surrendering power, even though interactions should be well-scripted. Defying authority tremendously empowers an individual, even in the ultimate act of surrender. On the other hand, emotions experienced by a dominant in taking power can also heighten the experience, and include a range of feelings from focusing total erotic attention on the needs of the submissive, to titillating guilt about indulging in taboo behavior.

Methamphetamine's impact on this cornerstone of desire is dramatic. Without drugs, the search for erotic power is expressed in the give and take between two people. One partner is giving and one is receiving; one partner is validating and one is being validated. Each is highly attuned to what is happening not only within themselves but with their partner. The intensity of this power exchange is such that many practitioners even describe it as a spiritual connection.

With methamphetamine, the experience of power exchange quickly changes from one of mutual interaction, in which the dominant and submissive represent a whole, to separate individuals (or more) focused much more selfishly on their own experience. While some claim that meth maintains a heightened sensory state in which they experience a strong bond with their sex partner, many more begin to experience fantasies characterized by exploitation of others or abuse of themselves. Meth seriously impairs one's ability to empathize and connect, which significantly increases the physical and emotional danger of the search for power under the influence.

One client of mine named Todd is typical. He is a white professional in his mid-forties who is very community-minded and has actively incorporated spiritual principles into his daily life, sincerely helping others and being generous with his time and resources. Todd's sexual template focused on younger men in their twenties, with whom he had several successful and loving long-term relationships. He was particularly disturbed by a meth-induced fantasy that involved him dominating others. This became prominent, and ultimately was the only way he could reach an orgasm.

> *"In the fantasy my boy and I are on my bed. We are both nude and watching porn. He attends to my sexual needs while feeding me hits from my meth pipe. While he's working on me, I make up elaborate stories describing how the two of us are going to travel across the country getting high on meth and seducing other young guys, ultimately forcing them to smoke meth with us, or injecting them, and getting off on perverting them. My boy admires my power and the two of us get aroused at the thought of dominating as many young, hot guys as we can. In the fantasy we become outlaws, just traveling, getting high, and force-feeding meth to boys until we die. And not just meth. We're both [HIV]-positive, and there's a reckless thrill at the thought of endangering them with unsafe sex, or even purposely infecting them."*

The cruelty of this fantasy was not lost on Todd, who in fact was quite traumatized by it. Many people using meth experience equally disturbing fantasies in which exploitation, or at least a total lack of empathy toward others, becomes the dominant theme.

It is not understood whether meth disinhibits the mind, thereby allowing existing dark fantasies to bubble up into consciousness, or whether meth chemically alters the nature of erotic fantasies, resulting in new extremely disturbing scenarios. While the mechanism is unclear, it is certain, at least in the realm of the search for power, that meth's role in reducing empathy results in fantasies that are highly disturbing.

Does meth's reduction of inhibitions increase the likelihood that the fantasy will spill over into murderous reality? There is no evidence of significant increased meth-driven rampages, although there is an abundance of proof that poor impulse control and a lack of empathy under the influence do result in harm. This is seen in the high level of child abuse, a rupture of the parent-child bond, in homes where meth is present, as well as in the aggressive carelessness of unsafe sexual activity.

Overcoming Ambivalence

The fourth cornerstone of erotic desire is overcoming ambivalence, which is much less intuitive than those already described. Unfortunately, it is a common experience to be hurt by those we love and upon whom we are, at least as children, dependent. As adults, this can take the form of attraction to emotionally unavailable individuals or, more destructively, to persons who are verbally, emotionally, or even physically abusive.

It is counterintuitive that we would be drawn to someone who could or has harmed us, but if erotic themes are understood in the context of neutralizing emotional pain by eroticizing aspects of that person or relationship, it becomes clearer. One type of couples counseling, Harville Hendrix's Imago Therapy,[5] utilizes this principle in helping individuals recognize that their ideal mate is a combination of traits, good and bad, of significant people in their early lives.

Everyone can describe an experience of being attracted to someone without really understanding the basis of the attraction. Imago therapy proposes that the person to whom we are drawn has some characteristics of the people who raised us, and we may not be consciously aware of these traits, but rather sense them. We are drawn to individuals who reflect positive characteristics of our caregivers. We are also drawn to individuals who remind us of someone who has harmed us in the past. We may be drawn to a stranger who we subconsciously sense could repeat that harm in an effort to finally re-enact that relationship and ultimately heal the wound. The problem is that this often results in rewounding.

Morin states[6] that the role of ambivalence is unrecognized because it is a transient feeling, largely disappearing by the time one is aroused. Unlike breaking taboos, which tend to heighten a sexual experience while one is engaged in the act, ambivalence adds to the buildup of sexual excitement preceding the encounter. Methamphetamine impacts our willingness to act on ambivalent attractions, and therefore results in increased physical or emotional harm. The case of one client, Neal, clearly illustrates this.

> *Neal is a gay black man in his mid-thirties, who was raised by his mother in the rural south after his father abandoned the family at an early age. He experienced significant hardships as a child as his mother struggled to maintain their home. She periodically fled, both physically and emotionally, and during those periods when she, "couldn't cope," would leave Neal and his sister with her mother and father, who was a conservative preacher. Neal's grandfather was verbally and physically abusive, conveying disgust at his own daughter and contempt for Neal and his sister. Neal left home as soon as he could get out, making his way to a large nearby city and supporting himself through hustling.*
>
> *Neal invested considerably in his own wellbeing, attending community college, working diligently, and eventually maintaining a good job and home. The one area of his life that remained unsatisfactory were his relationships. Neal got involved in several relationships that lasted three or four years, usually with older men who he later determined were emotionally unavailable. They did not communicate feelings with each other, and when the sex began to cool, the relationship failed.*
>
> *Neal experimented with drugs through his twenties but never considered them to be a problem until he encountered methamphetamine. He was introduced to the drug by Dave, a man in his*

late-forties who was already injecting meth when Neal met him. Neal states he was immediately drawn to Dave's powerful build, his tattoos and piercings, and the sex, which he described as the best of his life. Dave started injecting Neal with meth, and Neal reported that they had a highly erotic sex life. Dave demanded an open relationship to which Neal reluctantly agreed, believing that this was necessary to keep even a minimal amount of Dave's attention.

Their tumultuous relationship began to erupt into arguments that overflowed into physical violence, sometimes followed by more drugs and sex. This pattern continued until Neal stormed out and, determined to break his addiction to Dave, drove across the country and tried to re-establish himself in another city. He was able to maintain this fresh start for several months and get clean, but inevitably thoughts of Dave would creep in and he began to obsess about him all the time. They reestablished contact, and Neal moved across the country back to Dave. Their stormy relationship quickly picked up where it left off, and Neal soon had not only some new bruises, but also a full-blown meth habit and Hepatitis C. Once again Neal determined the only way he could survive was to leave, and get as far away as possible. Less than a year later he moved back to Dave for a third time. Finally, after nearly fatal health complications from high-risk sex and drug use, including a drug-resistant infection (Methicillin-resistant Staphylococcus aureus, also known as MRSA) from injecting drugs, Neal got into treatment and was able to maintain abstinence from meth and Dave for an extended period of time.

In therapy Neal was able to identify the ambivalence in his relationship with Dave. Rationally he knew Dave was destructive and harmful, but he was continually drawn back to him, hoping to receive nurturing and care from a man—something he had always desired. Meth exaggerated the whipsaw effect of Neal's experience through intense sexual and emotional heat that quickly transformed itself into ugly violence and the same cold contempt that Neal had experienced since childhood. As things worsened, Neal used meth less for sexual enhancement and more to numb the growing emotional pain that pushed him toward hopelessness and suicide. In Neal's case, ambivalence combined with meth nearly cost him his life.

Making Sense of Erotic Desire

Gay men are especially susceptible to separating parts of themselves, encouraged to do so not only by society but by self-preservation that ruthlessly suppresses urges which would invite disapproval. This splitting is maintained by powerful feelings, especially shame. Men learn as young children that attractions felt toward other men are wrong, and that expressing them would threaten relationships with key caregivers who are essential for survival.

Over time many men develop a protective duplicity that enables them to comfortably compartmentalize aspects of themselves. There is lust and love, good and bad, conformity and taboo. Most gay men identify with the well-behaved boy who is familiar to parents, teachers, and employers. Most gay men also recognize the other extreme that Guy Kettelhack[7] calls the beast: the lust driven, animalistic, objectifying, predatory sexual side that is hidden but universal. Strong barriers of shame and self-esteem keep these two divides cleanly separated.

Some gay men maneuver easily between the two, while some have more difficulty recognizing, let alone acting upon, the desires of the beast. Even fewer gay men have found ways to successfully allow these two identities to coalesce into one, struggling with basic acceptance of their non-conforming sexual drives. Others have had success adopting a more playful, accepting attitude about these two realms, easily flowing between their public persona and their private drives without a large energy expenditure on negative feelings such as shame or fear.

Many gay men who use methamphetamine (and other drugs) to enhance sex, experience the thrill of sharing lustful feelings with another person, and even acting them out. The drug's disinhibiting effects make such deep sharing far easier, resulting in a sense of intimacy that comes from the vulnerability of exposure combined with the thrill of revealing these fantasies to another person.

It is common for many men to mourn the sense of intense, interpersonal bonding when they give up methamphetamine. But this sense of connection need not be dependent on the drug. Authentic connection and healthy intimacy are created by allowing oneself to be vulnerable and visible.

Sex, then, becomes an opportunity to find and cultivate self-worth and love for oneself. Personal erotic scripts and themes derive from our life experiences and reveal much about our fears, needs, and capability to meet those needs. Approaching sex playfully (while keeping in mind personal responsibility to protect ourselves and our partners), is one of the most freeing experiences of a gay man's life.

Kettelhack likens these drives within a gay man to a volcano. We dance around the edge of the volcano, which is indeed explosive and dangerous. Some fall into it through excesses, others stay well back from its crater. Many men have found that the only way they can explore these volcanic summits is to release these urges through alcohol, methamphetamine, or other mood-changing substances and behaviors. These, of course, ultimately cause even more harm, reinforcing the cycle of shame. Exploration of this psychosexual territory is not easy or without risks, but with help and growing self-awareness many men have achieved both a drug-free life and an affirming sexuality.

Sex can heal core beliefs and attitudes through increased awareness and a desire to change. It is a powerful force of integration as lost pieces of ourselves are rediscovered, explored, and incorporated. As shame and vulnerability dissolve, choice and empowerment emerge.

The last two chapters have explored the psychological forces that create and fuel sexual desire in each unique individual. The next and final chapter in this guide to the sexual universe addresses fascinating discoveries about the brain. Its ability to constantly change and evolve sheds new light not only on the power of methamphetamine and other addictive behaviors to have physical impact, but also provides clues about the steps required for healing and recovery.

7

Sex and the Plastic Brain

During the last decade we have seen significant advances in our understanding of neuroscience and the processes by which our brains learn, adapt, and continually create new neural pathways. It was once believed that different parts of the brain had permanent, specific functions. While there are certainly various central locations for senses (such as vision, hearing, taste, and smell), the brain has much more flexibility in adapting to a situation or condition than was previously believed. With the advent of functional magnetic resonance imaging (fMRI) and other advanced technology, tests have been conducted on persons with various disabilities such as blindness to see how the brain compensates for such conditions. We are beginning to understand that the brain is plastic; that is, it continues to evolve and change in response to external stimuli. Someone who loses their eyesight will develop heightened awareness of other senses to compensate. Doidge, in his book *The Brain That Changes Itself*, notes that the brain can be viewed as very high-priced real estate. If one's vision becomes impaired, the parts of the brain that were utilized for sight will be reassigned to other functions. The brain is far too efficient to allow that space to go unutilized.

> **My sexual tastes and desires morphed into something unrecognizable.**
>
> —METH USER

Through constant adjustment, the brain remains efficient and powerful. Bundles of nerve connections called neural pathways develop as we encounter new experiences and learn new skills. They bind together certain situations and behaviors, resulting in a unique set of tastes, drives, and beliefs about ourselves and the world that become wired into our brains. Over the course of a lifetime, our brains have periods of extreme development (as in childhood) as well as shedding of pathways (during adolescence and, interestingly, after falling in love). This process, called synaptic pruning, allows the brain to remain highly efficient by eliminating its least-used pathways, releasing resources for more frequently-utilized brain processes. Throughout our lives, our built-in supercomputer is constantly adapting and adjusting to our tastes and experiences. If we take on novel activities such as learning a second language, our brain begins to provide resources to that effort, creating new neural connections that contribute to its ongoing vitality. On the other hand, if we fall into the same routines day after day, our brains become less engaged and stimulated. In essence, we become what we practice.

The brain is constantly rewiring its neural pathways through a variety of very complex mechanisms that we are only just beginning to understand. This feature, called plasticity, is a marvelous adaptive ability that creates huge complications as well. For example, addictions and other compulsive behaviors that are practiced hundreds or thousands of times create neural pathways that permanently change the brain. And it is neural plasticity that is responsible for hijacking the sexual desire of meth users by fusing meth and sex together. When such fusion occurs, getting clean may mean losing sexual desire along with the drug.

We are beginning to understand that certain situations, such as being extremely task-focused, enhance the development of these neural pathways. We need to continually keep our brain interested in order to keep it vital and engaged. The phrase "use it or lose it" is particularly apt for our brains. Neurologists recommend lifelong incorporation into our lives of novelty such as learning new information and skills, and conversely, avoiding falling into the same routines. Something as simple as different routes on the daily drive to work or school, for example, helps keep the brain vital.

Today, our brains are adapting to uncharted territory. Never before in the history of man have we seen the level of stimulation we are now witnessing. Preliminary studies with children born into the digital age reveal that their brain development and wiring are different than the neural connections of those who grew up in the analog world. Computers have brought other changes as well. Pornography and video games, along with other experiences that overstimulate the brain, create a form of hyperstimulation through which the brain is actually altered. Several areas of the brain are affected, including permanent and detrimental changes in the nucleus accumbens, which may be an actual biomarker of addiction.[1]

The use of meth and other mood-changing drugs contribute to these permanent changes in the physical structure of the brain. When someone constantly uses meth (or any drug), it causes an excess of neurotransmitters, particularly dopamine, that create pleasurable feelings. Because the brain is highly efficient, it slows down or stops its own internal processes for stimulating the release of the neurotransmitter once it begins to rely on external signals. In other words, the brain becomes dependent on these artificial inputs to function normally.

The same is true for other so-called "process addictions." These are behaviors like compulsive use of pornography, gambling, or credit card spending—repeated actions that result in the same type of brain changes. The good news for both chemical and process addictions is that most of these negative changes can be reversed with time and patience because of the brain's plasticity, but they must be overlaid with new habits consisting of repeated, healthier behavior.

Although brain plasticity and its consequent neural changes are highly complex processes, some basic concepts are vital in helping someone getting clean from methamphetamine understand what changes have occurred in their brain and how they recover from the drug, as well as reclaim healthy sexuality.

The Limbic System

To understand meth's effects on these processes, we have to dive deep into a set of structures in the brain known as the limbic system, or more informally, the primitive brain. This lies on the border between the central part of the brain and the outer part, called the cerebral cortex. We share the limbic system with all mammals. Sometimes called the emotional nervous system, it is responsible for emotions, motivation, smell, behavior, and long-term memory. Various structures of the brain make up the limbic system, including the amygdala, hippocampus, cingulate gyrus, the olfactory bulb, the fornix, and the septum. Closely connected, but not actually a part of the limbic system, are the thalamus, hypothalamus, pituitary, and the reticular formation.

While the limbic system is very complex, it can be generally stated that this part of our brain is responsible for the so-called "reward circuitry," the means by which the body ensures survival by rewarding (or making pleasurable) certain activities. This is primarily achieved by a chemical messenger that flows through the system, a neurotransmitter called dopamine. When the release of dopamine is triggered by certain activities or desires, we experience pleasurable feelings. Our bodies are designed to reward acts of survival like eating, sex, and even companionship by making those activities feel good through the release of dopamine, thereby ensuring continuation of the species.

Complications occur when we introduce other chemicals or activities that trick the brain into releasing excessive amounts of dopamine. When that occurs, we have a momentary rush of pleasurable feelings followed by a phase of low mood and frequently a strong craving for more. This is how we teach the brain to be addicted.

Dopamine

We are gradually beginning to understand the tremendous impact that various behaviors have on the physical structure and functioning of the brain itself. The limbic system, the deepest and oldest part of the brain, operates on the basis of pure emotion and instinct, with no time or date stamp on what it is experiencing and no ability to discern a memory, thought, or fantasy from what is real in the present moment. For example, a war veteran might have post-traumatic stress disorder caused by an explosion, a very real trauma that overwhelms the brain and its ability to process the experience. When an unrelated loud sound occurs in the present, far away from the battlefield, all the brain's sensory mechanisms alert the limbic system that a very real danger is present, and the body reacts accordingly, sending out commands to increase heart rate, release stress chemicals, flex muscles, and so on. The danger is not real, but the limbic system is like a controller sitting in a room with no windows, relying only on the input of various sensory mechanisms. All the dials are screaming "danger," and the limbic system responds.

The same ability to trigger excessive amounts of dopamine occurs with fantasy. The limbic system cannot differentiate between an actual person who heightens sexual desire and causes a physiological reaction, including a flood of dopamine, and the two-dimensional image on a computer screen or in a sexual fantasy fueled by copious amounts of methamphetamine. The limbic system only knows that it is getting signals that something very desirable is "out there," and it reacts accordingly by releasing pleasure-inducing dopamine. The limbic system registers such fantasies as real, and with continued use of the drug or pornography (or any addictive behavior), such excessive input becomes the minimal level of stimulation required. One website[2] described the use of Internet porn as a "dopamine machine." Amphetamines, and methamphetamine in particular, are equally potent in their ability to induce dopamine release.

Because of the brain's marvelous ability to adapt, it quickly determines that high levels of stimulation from meth or porn are now normal, and these levels become required to trigger the release of dopamine. In real world experience, this means that vanilla sex, human partners, or sex acts without drugs are no longer satisfying because the brain has learned to rely on superstimulation to function normally. Part of this adaptation is the physical reduction of the number of dopamine receptors on nerve cells, also known as sensitization. Bodywisdom.com compares this very effectively to a person's response when he or she is being screamed at. You cover your ears! The brain achieves this by reducing the number of dopamine receptors. Sensitization also results in the brain needing less and less of the stimulating drug or behavior to result in intense cravings.

The reduction in the number of receptors results in yet another phenomenon of addiction known as tolerance. In drug terms, this means that more of the drug is required to achieve the same effect. Because of the decreased number of dopamine receptors, more stimulation is necessary to result in an adequate release of dopamine flowing through these limited receptors.

Another feature of dopamine is its responsiveness to novelty. Because of the brain's plasticity, it quickly adapts to stimulus. This means that a fantasy that was exciting today won't suffice tomorrow, or that pornography that was titillating on one day won't produce the same level of excitement the next. Meth users frequently describe a phenomenon of increasingly dark sexual fantasies and risky behavior. As the brain continually adapts, this escalation is necessary to achieve the same amount of excitement and stimulation. To keep the flow of dopamine, many addicts describe behavior in which they cannot stop cruising online sex sites, or viewing pornography, or leave the bathhouse, because they are constantly seeking more stimulus and something even more exciting.

As this process continues, the brain's ability to create, combine, and shed neural pathways keeps pace. A common slogan heard in Crystal Meth Anonymous meetings comes straight from neuroscience: "What fires together, wires together." This process is a key factor in the experience of many meth users who require darker and more extreme sexual acts or fantasies. This accurately describes the process that occurs when neural transmission of dopamine becomes dependent on a meth-induced high (or other drugs as well) combined with sexual thoughts or fantasies. Remember, dopamine is the neurotransmitter that binds behaviors and rewards together. Pavlov's principle of a dog associating a ringing bell with food and inducing production of saliva is totally based on dopamine's ability to wire all those things together. For the meth user (and the porn addict), being in an addicted state, combined with sexual fantasies and behavior, will fuse these two together. In other words, the brain begins to combine sex and meth in such a way that one becomes dependent on the other. Simply stated, when someone stops using the drug (or porn), sexual desire often disappears right along with it.

This loss of sexual desire is a huge concern for recovering meth addicts, and results from the process described above. Before going on to describe how healing occurs, we need to take one detour in the sexual universe to describe an additional, common sexual complication resulting from tinkering with dopamine: trouble with erections.

Understanding Erections

As simple as it may seem when someone is young, healthy, and unaffected by the destructive changes described above, achieving an erection is a complex neurological process that can be undermined in several ways. Erections begin in the brain, which is often called our most important sex organ. Indeed, orgasms can be described as a "carefully orchestrated series of events controlled by the Central Nervous System."[3] Arousal may be initiated by physical stimulation of the genitalia, which is quickly taken over by the brain, or by purely psychological factors such as attraction to appealing partners or fantasy. In addition to such partners (or objects, in the case of fetishes), some people become exclusively dependent on complex sexual scripts for arousal. These scripts are described in previous chapters and are frequently problematic for methamphetamine users. In such cases, it is the psychological or emotional theme of the script (power, helplessness, victimization, etc.) that causes arousal.

Erections represent a balance between two opposing forces of the autonomic nervous system: exciting and inhibitory forces. The sympathetic nervous system (SNS) tends to inhibit (remember that vessels constrict during a sympathetic response, which can result from fear, use of amphetamines, and other factors) while the parasympathetic nervous system tends to promote excitation. The potent ability of the sympathetic nervous system to inhibit is illustrated when it is turned off, as occurs during rapid eye movement (REM) sleep. During REM, it is very common for men to have night-time erections because the effect of the SNS is limiting.

These two opposing forces can also be viewed as "exciting pleasure" and "satisfying pleasure." Exciting pleasure results from our anticipation and imagination and is largely dopamine related. Chronic use of amphetamines (cocaine or methamphetamine), as well as pornography, lowers the threshold at which the pleasure centers of the brain "fire," making them easier to turn on, and therefore easier to succumb to fantasies and cravings.

Inhibitory forces, on the other hand, are related to satisfying pleasure, which results in feeling calm and fulfilled. They are related more to endorphins (opiate-like chemicals). This typically occurs when needs are satisfied, such as after a big meal or after an orgasm. As mentioned before, many meth users report that the drug drives them to constant, almost frenetic arousal even after experiencing orgasm (or multiple orgasms) when they should be feeling relaxed. In such cases it could be hypothesized that the exciting forces induced by meth are simply overwhelming the fulfilled satisfaction that should result from sexual climax.

Regardless of the source of stimulus, when the brain is sexually aroused it sends signals via neurotransmitters such as dopamine to create an erection. The dopamine prompts other biochemicals such as nitric oxide and acetylcholine to cause the smooth muscles lining the penile arteries in the corpus cavernosum to relax, thereby allowing a stronger blood flow that creates an erection. Many men believe that testosterone is responsible for erections, however that hormone influences them only indirectly by stimulating the production of dopamine.

Current treatment of erectile dysfunction (ED) assumes, almost exclusively, that the problem is physiological in the penis. Drugs such as Viagra, Cialis, and Levitra (so-called PDE-5 inhibitors) work by slowing the degradation of the chemicals (nitric oxide, acetylcholine) that keep the blood vessels relaxed, which promotes good blood flow and results in a longer-lasting erection. Since these drugs only work locally in the penis and only during the final stages of a long neurological process that begins in the brain, they have no effect if there is no sexual desire in the first place. In other words, if there are no (or limited) arousal signals being sent from the brain, there will be no production of nitric oxide and acetylcholine, thus presenting no opportunity for the ED drugs to function.

The ED common to most meth users results largely from two sources. Meth itself causes the constriction of blood vessels resulting from the pseudoephedrine in the meth (the precursor of the drug itself). Erections cannot occur with overly constricted blood vessels. Pseudoephedrine dries a runny nose by constricting vessels and has the same constricting effects elsewhere in the body. If desire is creating stimulating signals but the blood vessels are constricting as a result of meth ingestion, the PDE-5 inhibitors may work to produce an erection.

The other (and probably more significant) cause for ED in meth users (and other addicts, including those who use pornography) lies not in the penis but in the brain, back at the source of desire and arousal. Through repetitive addictive processes (whether consuming meth while having sex or watching porn in a hypnotically-induced state) the neural pathways for sex and the altered state begin to consolidate. Many men who are abstinent from methamphetamine complain that even after several months they have no sexual desire. They often admit how difficult it is while masturbating to keep their thoughts and fantasies from returning to the same sexual templates that were inextricably intertwined with meth, even though they are clean. Thinking about these scenarios continues to reinforce the meth-sex neural pathways even without the chemical reinforcement of the drug. Improvement will not occur until these pathways wither from non-use and new ones are formed. Creating new fantasies by focusing on sensations or interaction with a real-life partner are ways to achieve this rewiring, although it is difficult. The old pathways containing the hot-button sexual scenarios are deeply grooved in the mind. It is very difficult to avoid slipping into them. For this reason, many people in the first months of recovery choose to be completely abstinent.

While our knowledge of the complex working of the brain is far from complete, we are beginning to understand other changes that occur with addictive processes. Eric Nestler[4] at the University of Texas has documented what has long been suspected: addictions create permanent changes in the brains of animals. Doidge[5] reported that Nestler's work showed that "a single dose of many addictive drugs will produce a protein called 'Delta Fos B' that accumulates in the neurons. Each time the drug is used, more Delta Fos B accumulates, until it throws a genetic switch, affecting which genes are turned on or off." In other words, permanent changes occur as Delta Fos B accumulates through the use of addictive chemicals. Once flipped, this genetic switch causes irreversible damage to the brain's dopamine system, resulting in that animal being much more prone to addictive behavior. This certainly appears to reinforce the commonly held belief that "once an addict, always an addict."

The next section of the book is designed to present various tools to help the recovering person on his path toward sexual health. It is important to keep in mind that this is a long and sometimes difficult process. Healing is not always smooth or comfortable. There will be days that seem like setbacks. Someone may trigger uncomfortable feelings that are difficult to manage, and on some days there may be nearly constant cravings to numb or escape. During other periods one may fall into dark and hopeless moods with no overt cause. Through all this it is important to keep the long view in mind. Recovering men will be employing the plasticity of their brains to rewire old, harmful connections and to build new skills as well as emotional resilience.

▪ PART III

RESTORING YOUR LIFE

8

The Recovery Process

Unlearning dangerous old behaviors and establishing new ones takes time and considerable effort, but it can be done. Recovery cannot be achieved without the help of others. Meth, like other drugs, is particularly isolating. Of course, this doesn't mean that meth users don't have abundant social contacts. Some clients of mine may have had hundreds (or more) sexual liaisons, but remained profoundly lonely and isolated. Recovery requires reconnecting with others in a meaningful way. This can be accomplished by attending self-help groups (such as Narcotics Anonymous, Crystal Meth Anonymous, or Alcoholics Anonymous). Other groups such as SMART Recovery provide an alternative (as well as a complement) to twelve-step groups. A degree of resistance is very normal at first, but I encourage people to force themselves to go and stay in meetings for a period of time. It is important to make a commitment for at least ninety days before declaring that "twelve steps just won't work for me."

> **After quitting I'm finally able to appreciate the little things in life—the stuff that made me happy before.**
>
> —METH USER

In addition to support groups, I believe professionally facilitated groups are important as well. Giving up meth requires considerable behavioral changes that involve not only the drug(s) themselves, but reinventing other activities like sex, self-care, and socializing. This process is characterized by addressing lifelong dysfunctional patterns that may include unresolved grief, shame, feeling unworthy, and a host of other issues which, unless corrected, will provide ample material for relapse. Trained facilitators guide this process, resulting in meaningful change of destructive thoughts and feelings as well as the teaching and reinforcement of new skills and behaviors.

Experience shows that all links to these drug-related people, places, and things must be severed. This may mean friends, sex partners, even lovers and husbands. It means giving up the computer (where this is not possible due to occupational necessity, clients have installed censoring software to prevent being drawn into cruise sites or pornography). It may mean changing e-mail and phone number contacts, becoming celibate for a period of time, changing patterns and routines, and sometimes even relocating to a new city where memories and potential cravings are not linked to every corner. It should be cautioned, however, that such a move can easily be driven by a "geographical cure," in which the recovering person mistakenly employs "magical thinking" and believes that simply relocating to another place will solve all their problems. As many people in recovery are well aware, problems accompany us wherever we go.

While recovery from any addictive substance or behavior is difficult, the recovery process for meth, with its intense mood-altering effects and its associated sexual problems, can be even more challenging. The toxicity of the methamphetamine molecule is a major factor. The flood of neurotransmitters released by meth, most notably dopamine, quickly depletes the brain, resulting in ongoing depression. While molecules of other drugs such as cocaine are quickly washed away, meth lingers on the receptor, ultimately destroying it. This results in an especially prolonged period of recovery as the brain literally "rewires."

Recovery is further complicated because meth is not usually consumed in isolation but rather with additional drugs, including the so-called club drugs (ecstasy, ketamine, GHB), resulting in a powerful constellation of addictive impulses. Further cementing this behavior in place are other concurrent compulsive behaviors. Among gay men who use methamphetamine, the most prominent of these behaviors is compulsive sex. This takes many forms, including promiscuity, pornography, and escalated sexual risk-taking, but it always includes an obsessive preoccupation followed by acting out in some way. Methamphetamine affects the same part of the brain involved in sexual pleasure, causing the drug high and sexual urges to "fuse." Consequently, this results in a stubborn pattern that hijacks sexual desire and pleasure and lays the groundwork for ongoing, intense cravings.

All of these factors create a formidable and often treacherous path to recovery from meth and its associated behaviors. The recidivism (relapse) rate for meth is high, and like all addictions, recovery is dependent on the delicate balance between costs finally outweighing the seductive appeal of the high. At some point, the consequences of lost jobs, financial stability, relationships, and even one's freedom after an arrest, begin to overshadow whatever pleasure is found through addictive behaviors. The healing process is not brief and requires patience and realistic expectations about gradual improvement. The brain can take up to eighteen months to recreate its dopamine transporter system (the neural pathways that allow dopamine to move from one nerve cell to the next). Without adequate dopamine, the world seems bleak and depressing. I have seen many clients successfully fight off meth cravings for months, yet still be unable to experience feelings of pleasure.

Managing cravings, the associations between the drug and behaviors, must be learned as part of the recovery process. People, places, and things that trigger an urge for the drug must be "unlearned" by not reinforcing them, and then must be overwritten by practicing new, healthier behaviors. Meth establishes powerful links between the pleasurable experience of the dopamine rush and almost anything else: a ringtone, a particular street where drug buying took place, signing into a sexual networking site, a bathhouse, even an attractive man walking down the street. An entire universe of personalized associations connecting the drug and other people, places, or things must be unlearned, a process that requires tremendous care and vigilance. Such is the power of these meth-based associations; their mere thought (such as planning to go to a sex club, or quickly checking a sex app such as Grindr or Scruff) creates a reaction as strong as if the behavior were taking place. Unfortunately, the great power of the mind to anticipate pleasure is turned against someone in recovery because such a trigger is inevitably followed by an overwhelming craving for the drug.

Stages of Recovery

Experience demonstrates that when one first stops using meth there is an initial phase of about two weeks that is characterized by intense cravings, a variety of psychological symptoms (including depression, anxiety, paranoia, and even some psychotic features such as hallucinations), as well as physical symptoms such as tremors, fatigue, and disrupted sleep. Most of these abate relatively soon, although a small minority of meth users continue to have disturbing thoughts and dreams for an extended period of time. Physical concerns related to chronic meth use include sinus infections, impetigo (a skin infection) and other skin conditions, weight loss, dehydration, as well as cardiopulmonary complications. Everyone getting clean should have a complete physical examination because some of these complications can be life-threatening and require intervention. This is especially true for anyone living with HIV/AIDS, since meth use nearly always disrupts adherence to antiretroviral medication. Resistance to antiretroviral medications may have occurred due to inconsistent adherence routines, so laboratory tests to determine the effectiveness of the current regimen may be required.

Most hospitals will not admit a methamphetamine user for detoxification, as such a level of care is not generally recognized as necessary for amphetamines because they do not directly cause the life-threatening complications and/or very severe withdrawal symptoms seen with alcohol or opiates. Yet, while there is no physical detox for amphetamines, significant psychological withdrawal clearly occurs during the first two weeks. Many users experience severe depression, suicidality, and/or psychosis. A psychological assessment should always be performed by a mental health professional to evaluate the need for safety (such as a psychiatric unit) for several days until there is evidence of stability.

The first weeks after giving up meth are characterized by severe mood swings, constant cravings, and a feeling of hopelessness that can be truly overwhelming. Systems should be put in place to provide support for individuals during this period because, for the reasons mentioned above, nearly anything has the potential to trigger a craving over which the person has very few defenses. It is telling that some of the best outcomes for meth users through these early and middle phases of recovery occur in people who are incarcerated, away from environmental cues and easy access to the drug.

Following the initial acute period, which lasts about two weeks, is a longer phase extending to about ninety days. During this time, the user begins the long process of unlearning old cues and establishing new routines. A new support system needs to be established, including peers who encourage the user through the many difficult periods.

At this time the recovering person will also need to start acquiring tools, skills, and insights that will help him/her on their journey back to health. This is complicated by the muddled thinking resulting from brain chemistry, which, through use of meth and other drugs, has become unbalanced. Concentration is often very poor, which interferes with any gains in insight. Even basic tasks such as comprehending the twelve steps and twelve traditions posted on the wall in meeting rooms may be difficult. I have had clients tell me that for months most writing seemed like "gibberish." Their brains simply couldn't make sense of the words.

Therapists dealing with meth addiction recognize this and often modify a traditional mainstay of psychotherapy called cognitive behavioral therapy (CBT). CBT relies on changing flawed thought patterns in order to produce healthier emotions and behaviors. CBT is very effective, but requires that the client be able to analyze thought patterns and substitute new ones. Recovering meth users, with a short attention span and poor verbal memory (comprised of memory or words and abstract language), often find this process difficult. For that reason, many clinicians simplify the process to "CBT light," wherein the basic concepts are maintained but with simpler structures, fewer words, and for a shorter period of time.

Interestingly, visual memory (a form of memory and processing relating to our visual experiences) seems less impaired by meth. Many clinicians integrate this into their interventions through the use of diagrams or the use of very visual language when describing concepts or giving feedback to the client.

This period of fuzzy thinking extends through ninety days and well beyond. In addition to daily support meetings, the most effective therapy interventions take into account the client's short attention span and the need to constantly resist cravings. Traditional treatment models such as intense hospitalization for detox or a twenty-eight day inpatient program are generally not considered effective for meth users. Clients simply don't benefit from or absorb the information and feelings resulting from such an intensive experience. Rather, the "best-practices" program design for methamphetamine utilizes a variety of shorter, evidence-based practices in an intensive outpatient setting, integrating users at different stages of recovery that continues for months.[1] This model of daily groups is difficult to replicate, but the principles of shorter duration, streamlined content, and reinforcement can be recreated.

The period around ninety days has long been a recognized benchmark in addictions. This is reflected in the slogans and structure of twelve-step programs, and is borne out in the experience of meth users as well. The period around ninety days represents a time of heightened risk for relapse. This may be due to the shifting pace of recovery from a sprint to a marathon, during which a solid recovery is developed. Fresh routines, new people, relapse prevention planning, and managing all kinds of feelings (both pleasant and unpleasant) need to be integrated.

Successfully navigating the sometimes treacherous waters after ninety days leads to a smoother period of personal growth. Cravings can occur any time, so one's guard should never be let down. After ninety days, new neural pathways begin to form whereby new routines replace old ones. Our plastic brains are working on our behalf to restructure and rewire as new behaviors become incorporated into our lives. For example, a chance encounter with a meth-using sex partner at a neutral place like the supermarket could trigger a powerful urge for the drug. Rather than entertaining the ensuing drug thoughts, the recovering person could immediately "switch gears" mentally and make a phone call to a member of his support group. Or he could practice some deep breathing for a few minutes, or recite elements of a gratitude list. All of these new behaviors start to overwrite the neural pathways that lead directly from a trigger to use of the drug.

One of the key difficulties with which people struggle during this period concerns emotions. Feelings and moods that had been numbed for months (and sometimes years) begin to reawaken and emerge. Frequently negative, these feelings are uncomfortable. Sadness, anger, fear, abandonment, and other potentially overwhelming emotions bubble up and demand attention. A lifetime's worth of unfinished business, lying dormant for years, usually begins to feel overwhelming. Recreational drugs are an effective means by which to numb, escape, or sometimes magnify feelings. Once these drugs are removed, there is no buffer between the user and raw emotions.

Many recovering addicts have few tools with which to deal with these emerging feelings. Indeed, the initial impetus toward drug use may have been created by painful emotions. I have worked with many men and women in early recovery for whom identifying even a basic feeling is a challenge. Sometimes they can only determine feeling "bad" or "good" (the former with much greater frequency). It is not unusual for someone to be unable to identify a feeling at all, but rather only be conscious of somatic symptoms such as a tightness in their chest, a pit in their stomach, or a constricted feeling in their throat. An essential task in early recovery is to learn how to identify those feelings, express them appropriately, and move on. For many, this is a challenge, but is a necessary one. Unaddressed feelings cause discomfort, which in turn leads to cravings and relapse. Chapter Ten is devoted to handling feelings.

Relapse

One aspect of the meth mystique that needs to be challenged is that there is no hope; that one is basically lost. This is simply not true. While recovery from meth is difficult, it is absolutely possible. The recovering addict must address certain key tasks, including giving up the behaviors that have become associated with the drug, learning how to manage feelings in real time (and clear out the backlog of emotional "unfinished business"), and addressing core issues that meth very effectively numbed or distracted from (such as shame, low self-esteem, or feeling socially disconnected, lonely, or unattractive).

One of the most discouraging aspects of meth use is its high rate of recidivism, the rate at which people use the drug again. All drugs present challenges for staying clean and sober, but meth is particularly difficult because of the way it attacks the pleasure center of the brain and how it converts almost any behavior—even the most innocent—into a potential trigger for the drug. Unlearning and undoing these associations takes time. Until alternative healthier behaviors take effect, the newly recovering person is at heightened risk for relapse.

It is important to acknowledge that many men and women successfully get over meth, although a newly clean person may experience "self-talk" that says otherwise. Recovering persons should listen for phrases like, "no one can," "never," or "always." These absolute terms represent erroneous thinking and lay the groundwork for relapse. I have had clients tell me with a straight face that literally everyone in the gay community uses meth, and that if someone says they don't, they must be lying. The men stating this "certainty" absolutely believed it, and it reinforced their conviction about the hypocrisy and shallowness in the community. It kept them bitter and angry, and most important, disconnected them from a support system that could potentially be helpful.

The truth is that nearly everyone in their drug-using circles may have indeed been using meth as well as other drugs. It becomes necessary, however, to view the community in its entirety. While the majority of gay men do not use meth, do not use club drugs, and are not living in a whirlwind of obsessive and compulsive self-destructive behaviors, people do generalize beyond their circle of acquaintances to the entire community. These views become an echo chamber of rationalization. "Everyone else is doing it." "This is normal—I'm no different than anyone else." Or, as one client stated after his first arrest, "I'm not so bad—you should hear about my friend who got arrested *again*."

Sometimes an arrest or another case of syphilis (or any one of a number of things that actually helps someone hit rock bottom) is useful. It provides a brief window of clarity; an opportunity for perspective during which one escapes the vortex of the drug and sees the patterns in their stark truth. It is during this window that a strong commitment to recovery, or at least to consider getting help, is forged.

Relapse occurs when this clarity, for a variety of reasons, becomes clouded again. Those erroneous beliefs ("stinking thinking" in recovery parlance) begin to take hold. One can tell oneself:

"It seems that everyone is using drugs again."
"I'm stronger now, maybe I can handle it."
"I need to get laid. I'll be able to say no if someone offers me drugs."

This process happens gradually. People may begin finding fault with their support groups, feeling put upon to do the hard work necessary for the reinvention of self in recovery, or beginning to have little secrets that at first seem relatively harmless. All this happens in the context of a chorus of small but persistent cues that occur every day. Reminders of the drug can pop up at any place and any time, but these are often effectively handled by staying away from people, places, and things. Once in a while, someone's history intrudes itself into the present moment, as has occurred when someone gets a text from an old using buddy even after changing their phone number, or seeing an old trick in the supermarket, or even worse, walking into a Crystal Meth Anonymous meeting and finding several people with whom they have partied.

Sexual Recovery

When meth and sex are combined, the brain learns (and begins to expect) that these two stimuli occur together. After a period of practice, the two become undifferentiated. If one takes away meth, sexual desire goes with it. Michael Merzenich,[2] a neuroscientist at University of California Berkeley, calls this phenomenon in which two previously distinct brain functions fuse, as in the case of meth or porn and sex, a brain trap. The technical name for this is LTP, or long-term potentiation. LTP is a basic component of the brain's ability to learn. When such fusing is undesired, it is called a brain trap.

There is a second phenomenon in which fused pathways are redifferentiated. This is called long-term depression (LTD), which has nothing to do with mood-related depression. The process of unlearning or separating these pathways is not well understood, but it is possible because of the brain's plasticity. Research is being undertaken with various biochemicals, such as oxytocin, that promote "unlearning," although practical application of this work is not yet available.

One common problem in attempting to unlearn unwanted associations (or redifferentiate them) is that the more a person tries to release these associations, the deeper they become. Doidge[3] refers to this phenomenon as focal dystonia, normally considered a muscular disorder typically seen in musicians, dentists, and other occupations with extensive hand use. A musician, for example, might lose the ability to move individual fingers separately. In attempting to redifferentiate them, Merzenich[4] and his colleagues discovered that it was unproductive to try to move the fingers separately but rather to relearn how to use their hands as they did as babies.

Doidge reports[5] on a treatment protocol by one of Merzenich's colleagues for treating guitarists with focal dystonia. The first step was to stop playing guitar for a while, which weakened the merged brain map. The next step was to hold an unstrung guitar for several days, followed by playing with a single finger on a single string, in turn followed by a second finger on a second string. With time and patience the fused pathways will eventually separate into two distinct maps once again.

Can this same procedure be applied to meth and sex? What are the lessons for redifferentiating a brain map for sexual desire and a drug-induced state that have fused? The long process (up to eighteen months) of restoring the brain's dopamine transporter system caused by the destructive nature of the meth molecule has been described in this book. A similar process, measured in months, is necessary to allow sexual desire to separate from a drug-dependent state and for the user to regain prior levels of sexual desire and functioning.

The first step is allowing the brain to "reboot." Just as the guitarist described above needed to stop playing guitar in order to weaken the merged brain maps, the newly clean meth user needs to step back from sex. This means total abstinence, including from masturbation. This phase does not last forever, but it is a necessary step in loosening the fusion between sex and intoxication. I have found that most meth users are actually relieved to abstain from sex for a period of time simply because almost any sexual thought results in intense drug cravings, which often leads to relapse. By eliminating sex from their lives, these men buy themselves some much-needed time and relief from the constant barrage of distracting sexual impulses.

This period of sexual abstinence, in which the fused neural pathways are not reinforced, allows another neurobiological process to take place. This is the quite miraculous process of our neurological system to develop new dopamine receptors as our brains readjust from the destructive "screaming" level of stimulation to a more modulated and normal one. This takes a long period of time and is not a smooth, linear process. There will be good days and bad days, and at times recovery will mean having to focus almost minute-to-minute on staying clean and avoiding thoughts that trigger cravings.

Sexologists know that sexual templates, once formed, do not disappear. Expansion of elements occurs, but the old destructive ones remain, albeit hopefully dormant. With time (and without reinforcement) they will fade from prominence, but they will not be gone. This means that constant vigilance is required to avoid "lighting up" those old drug-related portions of one's template.

Just as the guitarist introduced first one string and then another, the recovering addict will eventually decide to reintroduce sexual behavior. The timing of this decision is highly individual and depends on the level of cravings, support, and prior levels of healthy sexuality, including intimacy skills. Masturbation is the first step toward integrating sexual behavior. It is vital to focus on stimulating fantasies of a real person that have virtually no meth-related content, or that follow none of the sexual scripts that might have evolved during one's drug-using career. If one masturbates to familiar drug-related scenarios that were previously associated with meth (or any drug), even without actually ingesting the drug itself, the map will remain vital and strong. No progress will be made.

Many clients abstaining from meth begin to worry that they will never have sexual sensations again. Many men typically say that if they don't resort to the old fantasy scenarios, they find nothing stimulating. But with time, and the conscious development of new neural pathways, those in recovery regain a healthy connection with their sexuality. Time and creativity are necessary.

It is important not to try and replace "meth-sex" with some other version of hyperstimulated arousal in which one's partner (or partners) is objectified through various fantasies acted out without the drug. This simply won't work. Many men at first feel the need to grieve the intensity of such self-described "pig" behavior, feeling doomed to an unfulfilling life of uninteresting sexual connection. Many clients have, in early recovery, sought to recreate the intensity of "party and play" sex without the "party," but quickly find that pornography, casual hookups, bars, fetishes and any other reminder of meth-associated activity soon trigger drug cravings. If they are honest with themselves, they often admit that such sexual acting out lost its erotic appeal long ago, and had become an exercise in empty physical acts that left them neither sexually satisfied nor emotionally fulfilled. In fact, it often wrenches them away from an authentic connection with both their own feelings and those of their partner.

Once one chooses to begin masturbating in this "remapping" phase, I suggest that they try to focus on physical sensations. What kinds of touch are pleasant or unpleasant? What parts of the body enjoy stimulation, and particularly, what kinds of touch? By focusing on body sensations one is less inclined to slip back into the deep grooves of the unhealthy fantasies and scripts. It is not unusual to be unable, at first, to achieve orgasm. If that is the case, I advise one to be patient and just enjoy the sensations as they explore their body.

If the person has a partner with whom they can practice touch, there is an excellent exercise for couples developed by the well-known sex therapists Masters and Johnson. This process is called "sensate focus," and is an exploration in which one partner takes a turn being the "pleaser" and one being the "receiver." A vital element of this exercise (at least in the beginning phases) is that touching the genitalia is not included in the exercise, in fact, it is "prohibited." The point is not sexual orgasm but rather to discover in yourself and your partner new erotic zones and preferences for styles of touch. This discovery process creates new pathways that replace the old, unhealthy ones.

Over time one can reincorporate masturbation and orgasm, and then begin to develop deeper interpersonal connections, all the while avoiding any addiction-tainted sexual brain maps. Many men discover that, far from missing the intensity of meth-sex, they are capable of intimacy that includes not only physical expression, but emotional (and some say spiritual) elements as well. The ability to connect with another human at multiple levels is far more satisfying and sustainable than drug-dependent sexual acting out.

It cannot be overemphasized that throughout this process it is critical that old sexual scripts be left behind. They will lurk in the corners of one's mind and will try to entice one back to old fantasies and scenarios. They must be ignored and left to wither. It is a bad idea to attempt to *not* think about them. Anyone who has tried to avoid concentrating on something knows that the object of avoidance remains a central focus of one's attention. It has been said that the brain doesn't understand negatives or the word "not." If a concept is present, even if framed with the notion that one is trying NOT to think about it, that concept remains energized.

It is a far better strategy to replace those thoughts and scripts that dwell inside the mind with experiences that connect one to the real, external world. That is why a focus on physical sensations is helpful. The value of this external focus becomes clear when one is connected to an intimate partner, utilizing empathy and an awareness of giving and receiving with another person. This experience is far removed from the self-contained drug scripts in which a partner is simply a prop in one's fantasy. True intimacy requires a connection with another person at multiple levels that can be truly more profound and pleasurable than an intense meth-sex experience.

Many LGBT persons have sought and struggled to achieve a deeper level of intimacy without the use of alcohol or other mood-altering drugs or behaviors. Intimacy without these protective barriers is intense and uncomfortable, but if one approaches it slowly and with a gentle, compassionate attitude for oneself and one's partner, a significant bond will develop.

Even with a careful approach, developing such intimacy requires time, patience with self, compassion for all concerned, and vulnerability. Many of my clients find that such one-to-one intimacy is far too overwhelming, so they begin by developing their connecting skills with peers and support groups. These experiences are invaluable in helping them begin to emerge out of themselves and form relationships with others. Allowing someone else to act as a mirror for us can, at first, result in a bit of terror, as well as its closely related cousin, thrill.

As one begins to feel more secure about peeling off layers of vulnerability, many find themselves starting to act in a more spontaneous and playful manner. This lightness serves as a kind of antidepressant during this period (although actual antidepressant medication may be indicated as well). It feels exhilarating to realize that one can have pleasure, connection, and excitement that result from healthy activities without relying on substances or behaviors that alter one's mood.

With time, such practices help connect the recovering person with their own long-forgotten inner selves. Awareness of core beliefs, along with working toward resolving old emotional wounds, results in a shift of consciousness that profoundly changes one's relationship with oneself and the world. Over time there is no longer a need to numb and avoid old psychic pain, or to superstimulate dopamine production through intense emotions such as risk, shame, or anxiety. Instead, one begins to fill that void with positive feelings about oneself and authentic human connection. This is that path to true intimacy.

If one is to reconnect with the world and a healthier existence, it is impossible to totally separate from relapse triggers. One needs to make a daily commitment to the recovery process, be constantly vigilant, and have an active relapse prevention plan. Such a plan simply anticipates what has the highest risk to go wrong and creates a strategy or strategies to address it. If free time is determined to hold high risk for drug cravings, efforts should be made to schedule activities to ensure constant engagement. If a situation that will trigger a drug craving is to be encountered, such as getting blood drawn at the doctor's office, then a list of people to call (complete with phone numbers) should be readily available, or better yet, a friend should be asked to accompany the person in recovery.

My client Ted was a flight attendant whose normal work routine took him on four-day trips. Because of drug testing and being conscientious, he had little trouble staying clean while on the road. He was out of drug circles, had few stimuli that triggered a craving, and simply believed it was wrong to use drugs when the safety of other people was in his hands. His return home after a trip presented great challenges, however. He knew that he would have several days off in a row, and he had heard that meth takes about seventy-two hours to clear the body (should he be drug tested). He knew from experience that he needed at least twenty-four hours to recover from a drug run, which provided time to get some sleep, rehydrate, and re-nourish before leaving on another trip. All of those considerations gave him a window of about thirty-six to forty-eight hours to use from the moment he walked out of the crew area at the airport until the time he knew he needed to begin cleaning up to start his work cycle again.

While traveling, Ted began to obsess about his arrival home and plan for his days off. Such anticipatory thinking is typical. He began planning what he was going to do, who he might encounter, and where he might meet them. Eventually he started using the Internet to try and arrange hook-ups before he even landed at home. "Gay men are so unreliable," he said. "We make a date and they never show up... I don't have patience for such time-wasters!" This anticipation grew more intense on the last day of his trip. By the time he got home, his brain was already hungering for the drug to soothe the cravings that had been stoked by all the anticipatory thinking.

Over a period of months, however, Ted found it more and more difficult to resist the risk of using. Meth use is characterized by lines being drawn and crossed, boundaries established and broken, and promises to oneself being made and then tossed aside. Despite increased struggle with cravings, Ted was ultimately able to break these patterns. His hard work paid off.

It was important for Ted's relapse plan to focus on managing his time off, particularly that high-risk time when he first got home. He knew that he would put his entire job at risk if he used the day before going back to work, so after a certain point during his time off, the pressure to use diminished. Ted's relapse prevention plan thus focused on those critical thirty-six hours. One of the most essential things was formulating a plan for his time. Too much time, especially periods when he was unaccountable to anyone, was a dangerous thing. He knew he must have some commitment or an event scheduled on the evening he arrived home. He complained (even whined) that he was tired when he got home and needed to be free of any commitments. When it was pointed out that he somehow found the energy to get online and find tricks, or go to a bathhouse, even he had to laugh in self recognition.

Ted's relapse prevention plan involved making appointments for his crucial first and second nights at home. This was critical because it made him accountable. He couldn't just disappear at this time of very high risk. This required planning for things such as laundry and grocery shopping, which he admitted often were deferred in lieu of sexual hunting.

This simple measure, along with Ted's willingness to actually follow through, made an important difference in his ability to remain clean on his days off. In addition to simply making plans for his free time, Ted took other steps that enhanced his ability to stay clean. For example, he avoided risky situations. For him, that meant avoiding any extended period online, where he previously had spent hours surfing for sexual and drug liaisons. Because he needed to arrange his work schedule online, Ted asked a friend to install software (like a parental control software) that made it impossible for him to access these triggering websites. Could he have defeated these security plans? Yes, of course. With willfulness and some effort, Ted would have been able to overcome any of these precautions that were designed to simply slow down the time between initial thought and the trigger, which would lead to actual use. The key ingredient that made his relapse prevention plan effective was willingness.

Ted took other steps, such as changing his mobile number so that he no longer received texts from former users. He stopped associating with drug acquaintances, which actually created a huge hole in his social network. At first Ted complained that all his friends were swept away along with meth, but he soon realized that they had never truly been friends at all. Not one of these "friends" ever called unless they wanted to use drugs. Indeed, many of them had been around only when Ted provided drugs. When that stopped, they disappeared.

Ted found that one of the more challenging aspects of staying clean was boredom. He realized he had expended a great amount of time and energy fantasizing about using, planning for the use, obsessively trying to find sex and drug partners, actually hooking up, and then recovering physically, mentally, and emotionally. That cycle literally filled up all his time off. Once he extracted himself from that whirlwind, he found that he had a great deal of time on his hands. At first he was encouraged to use this time by going to recovery meetings. As he became more stable, he was able to seek out additional activities where he could socialize in healthy ways.

Although the cravings never totally disappeared, Ted was able to experience periods when he didn't think about the drugs or get triggered. As the pull of the drugs diminished, Ted began the long and slow process of rebuilding his life. He got a thorough physical examination to assess for any long-term impact of his drug use. He was fortunate in that he escaped permanent damage, such as pulmonary hypertension or acquiring a drug-resistant sexually transmitted infection. He utilized his recovery programs both as a vital support system and as a pool from which to derive new acquaintances and friends. He recognized that a twelve-step program was not psychotherapy, and after a period of some months, decided to find a counselor with whom he could work on long-standing issues such as loneliness and fear. He had been experiencing these negative feelings more strongly since giving up the drugs. He understood there was no longer a buffer between these emotions and his awareness, and that he needed tools to handle them.

One challenging problem remained, however, and it caused Ted a great deal of concern. That problem was sex. As with many other users of methamphetamine, he discovered that his sexual desire and functioning had been damaged by his drug use. In the first months without meth he discovered that he had no sexual desire at all. He actually felt relief about this, since in the past, his heightened sex drive drew him back into sexual networking sites and using drugs. Without such desire, he simply didn't have to deal with it. But after five or six months of clean time, Ted began to worry that his sexual desire wasn't going to come back. He could reawaken it if he thought about some of the sexual experiences or fantasies he had while using meth, although he knew that was a treacherous path. He began to be concerned that healthy sexuality would elude him.

Ted's experience is typical of the recovering meth user. In many cases, sexual desire has been hijacked by the meth. The brain has been taught very specific arousal patterns without which there seems to be no sex drive. Some men try to recreate the drug-induced sexual stimuli without the drug. Others hold out, trying to banish the meth-sex fantasies from their minds, and often can only last a limited period of time before relapsing, often falling into a cycle of frequent use and increasing shame and despair.

Ted decided that since he had little libido he would just put sex on the shelf for three months. This removed the tension he felt around the issue. Even as his body began to readjust to life without stimulants, Ted noticed that his sex drive remained dormant. He accepted this for a period, but after about six months he became increasingly concerned. He could stimulate himself through masturbation, but it seemed the only way he could achieve orgasm was to fantasize about some meth scene.

He instinctively knew this was dangerous because it once again brought cravings back to life. When Ted masturbated he was careful to avoid his old "hot button" fantasies. He focused on physical sensations or new erotic attractions that were dissociated from any connection with drug use or the erotic scripts that evolved with meth. At first he found this difficult. His mind wanted to lead him back to those old scenarios. If he couldn't resist, he stopped so as not to reinforce them. Ted even found it useful to think back on what had stimulated him before he ever picked up drugs, and to recharge the erotic appeal of those old memories.

Very gradually, Ted was able to begin to achieve orgasm while masturbating without being triggered. He really missed the physical connection with other men, but feared losing control with another person. He also found that the idea of sex without simultaneously using alcohol or drugs was frightening. He didn't know how to go about meeting someone. He knew any websites would trigger drug cravings, and he avoided getting involved with friends in twelve-step meetings.

Ted fought boredom by volunteering for a social service agency. This both filled his time and distracted him from his anxiety about sex and intimacy. It was here he met someone with whom he felt there was a possibility for some deeper involvement. The man had no drug history and, as they got to know each other, Ted felt increasingly comfortable with him. They went out to dinner several times, which ultimately led to a sexual connection.

Ted was honest with his new friend about his sexual history, and, by mutual agreement, they slowly explored intimacy with each other. When Ted was feeling overwhelmed, or not feeling any desire, he expressed this to his friend. Ted began to trust this man and found that new "green shoots" of attraction were beginning to form. Ted was working hard in his program of recovery to address old self-doubts and unrealistic fears, and in his interaction with his new friend he was able to explore new patterns as he gradually developed an awareness of both himself and his ability to connect with someone else. Ted was the first to say that this was not an easy or a simple process, but he did admit that one year into recovery he was well on the road to creating an active portion of his sexual template that was untainted by drugs and provided him both erotic stimulation and the satisfaction of interacting with another man at multiple levels, both physically and emotionally.

While Ted was able to begin healing physically, emotionally, and sexually, he inevitably encountered barriers to his growth that were deeply rooted in his past. These involved beliefs about himself that had influenced behaviors his entire life, including feeling victimized, feeling unworthy, and as a result, avoiding unpleasant emotions or situations. Anyone reclaiming their life from substances or addictive behaviors needs to begin healing at a deeper level in order to sustain their recovery. These essential skills for healing old wounds are described in the next chapter.

9

Healing Old Wounds

While the most important initial task for any user is to get clean from the drug, it is the identification and resolution of how emotions are managed that will create a foundation for a solid and long-lasting recovery. In this chapter we probe more deeply into some of the underlying psychological aspects of that perfect storm, in which methamphetamine and other recreational drugs merge with lifelong personality characteristics and situations to create intractable and destructive patterns. These typically provide users with a mental portal through which to escape uncomfortable emotions altogether, or they fuel erotic fantasies in which feelings of failure and unworthiness are transformed into sensations of power and invincibility.

> **Being sober is tremendously satisfying, but my deeper recovery has been about overcoming depression and working through lifelong personal issues.**
>
> — METH USER

Here are a few examples of how old methods for coping with distressing emotions undermine recovery:

Derrick, an African American man from Atlanta, had been living with HIV for nearly twenty years. He used meth periodically and, when he did, he spent days seeking out high-risk, condomless sex. After months of such partying, Derrick was told by his doctor that he had contracted hepatitis C. He heard the doctor's words, but had virtually no emotional response. Sitting in the doctor's office he could only think of how soon he could get home and slam some tina.

Derrick's old method for dealing with fear had been automatically triggered. The most effective means he had ever known for handling emotional discomfort was to numb it out, pushing it as far from consciousness as possible.

Robert, an attorney from Miami, was arrested as he left the bathhouse. The police had obviously been waiting for him, and he panicked that his whole world was about to collapse. As he shook and sweated profusely, the cops proposed a deal. They told him that if he went back inside and purchased more meth from his dealer, they would acknowledge his cooperation in court. He quickly agreed and returned inside, after which the police immediately arrested the dealer. When he was finally at home, despite what had happened, he could only concentrate on trying to score some more meth as soon as possible.

Robert was angry that he had been set up, and that his behavior, in turn, resulted in someone else's arrest. Having never been able to handle anger, he turned the feelings inward. He numbed himself through substance abuse and acted out his frustration through sex.

Steve, an architect living with HIV for ten years, was in a haze. After using meth for nearly five days, he had barely slept. He only wanted to slam some tina, go online, fantasize about sex, and maybe masturbate. He didn't even want actual sex—he was long past real-time hookups. After a weekend of seclusion doing just that, his penis was red and sore. He didn't care. His mind could only focus on sexual desire.

Steve had become addicted to the trance-like, altered state of computer pornography. Meth was central to fueling the erotic fantasies that helped him occupy an altered mental space and, at least temporarily, escape emotional pain.

Cognitive Escapism

The term "cognitive escapism" has been used to describe the need to find relief from disturbing thoughts and feelings related to HIV.[1] It is a perfect description for the actions of many gay men who use methamphetamine and hold a variety of beliefs about themselves, among them:

I'm not attractive enough.
I no longer have enough physical or sexual energy.
I am not young enough.
I am no longer a part of anything.
I have no future.

Such beliefs are as emotionally painful as any physical illness, and, like people seeking relief for physical pain through opiates, many people find that meth (and other recreational drugs) provides equally effective temporary relief from emotional pain. They literally flee their discomfort by using drugs while, of course, creating a plethora of other problems that inevitably undermine any sense of relief. Whether as a result of living with HIV, childhood wounds, a variety of other painful issues that have been ignored or buried rather than resolved, or sometimes simply boredom, painful feelings create an overwhelming sense of emotional discomfort that many people simply want to numb.

Formative Experiences that Lead Toward Addiction

Shame

Shame is perhaps the most prominent emotion experienced by gay men. This feeling is taught to us at an early age, and from many sources. Our parents, siblings, and childhood peers may shame us, sometimes without knowing it. The media and religious institutions are also harshly critical and condemning. Children are defenseless to resist because they are hard-wired to accept as true anything that an adult tells them. If we are told that we are bad, sick, inadequate, play like a girl, or anything else that instills a kernel of self-doubt, we accept it as the truth. These beliefs persist in our subconscious long after we grow up, and although we sometimes consciously refute those negative statements ("I am a strong man"), remnants of such shame linger even in the most evolved person.

When we are bullied, joked about, outed by others before we are prepared, or are diagnosed with a serious illness like HIV, these old kernels of shame are activated. The message is the same, whether they originated with our parents, the church, newspapers, television, or the Internet: *I am flawed.* People react in different ways to this disturbing belief about themselves. Some rebel, although this doesn't necessarily resolve the underlying conviction and related feelings. Some withdraw and hide, creating secrets to which they devote large amounts of psychic energy. Others simply numb the pain through the use of mood-altering drugs or behaviors. None of these coping mechanisms effectively rid us of shame; they only serve to drive us deeper into problematic behaviors and widen the gulf between our conscious adult selves and the wounded inner child that remains inside.

Shame provides both a powerful vehicle for the initial creation of addictive patterns and the impetus for their continuation. The underlying conclusion of shame is, *"I am flawed"* and, *"I can't allow the world to know the real me."* Gay men often carry this belief from an early age. They know intuitively that their innate attraction to men, even before understanding any sexual element to these feelings, is perceived to be wrong, sick, and even dangerous. As children they often have no other way to address these feelings except to bury or disconnect from them. Thus, from a very young age and literally driven by a need to survive, gay men learn to create a public "false self" for public consumption along with a private and secret inner world.

In his excellent book, *The Velvet Rage: Overcoming the Power of Growing Up Gay in a Straight Man's World,*[2] Alan Downs describes the long-term impact of shame. He divides this lifelong process into three stages, the first of which he calls "overwhelmed by shame." During this phase, gay men, unlike their straight peers, are prevented from developing a healthy emotional state because they feel unloved and flawed. The young gay boy begins to fake being straight, and any validation he receives flows to this false persona rather than his authentic self. Downs describes the frustration created by this process as resulting in rage, which can further push people away. The young gay man hides his anger in a "velvet glove," being a gracious friend and lover but one who is extremely sensitive to the slightest invalidation.

Down's second stage is "compensation of shame," where addiction begins to play a role. This is usually the longest phase and persists even though someone comes out as gay. A young gay man will compensate for shame by becoming the very best at whatever he does to reduce feelings of inferiority. This may be through material acquisitions, a perfect body, worldly sophistication, or even numerous sexual conquests. Despite his successes, the gay man is left feeling unfulfilled because the validation is still perceived to be inauthentic. During these times, gay men are particularly vulnerable to addictive processes, whether to further excite, ignite fantasies, or just to numb uncomfortable feelings.

The third and final phase of Down's model is "discovering authenticity," which usually occurs later in life as the gay man begins to seek and find real meaning, purpose, and integrity. Ironically, this is often the least visible stage, as such men typically withdraw from bars, clubs, and the social scene, creating a misperception in the community that such role models are lacking or don't even exist.

Of course, there are other sources of shame, including secrets in one's family of origin, abuse of various forms, body shame, other addictions in the family, financial issues, and almost any number of other concerns. If any of these are kept secret, they contribute to the maintenance of a false exterior self that is hiding inner feelings of fear, hurt, and anger. It is this gap between inner and outer lives that creates space for emotional pain, which must be dampened or numbed. In other words, addictive behaviors become a way to cope with the struggle between a person's authentic and false selves. In a sense, addiction can be seen as a form of dissociate disorder, in which one "disconnects" from traumatic or painful feelings. Drugs, behaviors, or even people are compulsively used to soothe the emotional pain caused by that breach between false and authentic selves. This behavior is, essentially, a very destructive form of self-medication. Ironically, by trying to escape these uncomfortable feelings, addictive behaviors actually perpetuate them by reinforcing the shame. Shame thus becomes an essential building block in the creation of a failed relationship with oneself.

Amphetamines (such as cocaine and methamphetamine) hold a particular appeal as antidotes to shame. This is because the experience of shame creates a form of emotional shock, a dissociative episode in which one disconnects from feelings. Although such dissociation is, at its most basic, one of the body's mechanisms for self-preservation, it is destructive when one disconnects from feelings because the emotions then become frozen and unexpressed.

As we have seen, shame at an early age provides a cornerstone for the development of an unhealthy relationship with oneself. Through a variety of early life experiences and insights, both overt and covert, a young child begins to form core beliefs about him or herself, which, unless changed, persist and inform behavior over the course of a lifetime. As adults, such beliefs frequently guide decision making, responses to stressful (both positive and negative) situations, and self-concept. Typically these include beliefs about oneself such as: *"I am unprotected," "I am unlovable," "I am flawed," "I can't handle this feeling,"* or *"I am powerless."*

Children react in certain ways as a result of these beliefs. For example, if they believe they are unprotected, they may decide never to take the risk of expressing their true feelings or being spontaneous. If they believe they are unlovable, they may decide that they need to work extra hard to earn someone's love. They may become a rescuer or a caretaker, and at some point will probably become unaware even of their own needs. A young man who feels flawed may strive to create a false self that tries to be perfect, perhaps physically by spending hours at the gym (and taking steroids) or by becoming intolerant of criticism. Someone who believes they can't handle feelings will eventually not even try, finding that mood-altering substances and self-destructive behaviors create at least a temporary reprieve from the discomfort of painful emotions. Finally, someone who feels powerless may try to affiliate with someone who can protect (or even control) them, or may strive to accumulate wealth or prestige to combat feeling ineffectual.

All of these long-standing beliefs and decisions about ourselves, made as a result of pivotal moments in our young lives, operate silently in the background unless they are made conscious and then changed. Despite being rooted in the past, they very much affect our present day decisions and relationships. I liken them to software that is unseen but guides virtually every aspect of a system's operations. Unless the negative beliefs and decisions are identified and corrected, they persist and continue to create undesired outcomes. It is these false beliefs that explain why people work very hard at changing external circumstances only to find themselves repeating the same behaviors and situations, seemingly endlessly. These invisible forces go a long way toward explaining repetitious and destructive behavior, which is discouraging for an individual and everyone around them.

Addictive behaviors, whether with substances or "process addictions," such as compulsive sex or pornography, typically work in two ways. They either provide a distraction from painful feelings, or they numb the emotional pain caused by these old wounds and their present day manifestations. Until we correct these false beliefs and their accompanying behavioral decisions, and then heal the wounding we have experienced, we are susceptible to the pull of addictive behavior.

Childhood Abuse

Rare is the child who emerges from early life without experiencing wounding of some sort. Being raised by others—each of whom has their own wounds, issues, and triggers—will inevitably lead to further emotional burdens imposed on the developing child. These may be relatively benign, such as a cross word or not giving/receiving enough attention. They can also be more overtly hostile, such as not encouraging creativity or actually discouraging it by being overly critical or disinterested. They can also cross all of these lines and become abusive, which will severely impact even the most resilient child. Abusive behavior takes many forms, including physical, emotional, intellectual, and spiritual abuse. In any of these manifestations, a child has few protections and is especially vulnerable to those persons charged with protecting him or her.

A history of abuse or trauma puts a child at much greater risk of developing addictive behavior as an adolescent or adult. Surviving an abusive childhood means putting one's own feelings aside, becoming invisible, or doing whatever is necessary to guarantee the love and support of one's caretakers. Long after the abused child grows up and is no longer dependent on adults for survival, these beliefs operate in the background and affect behavior. They contribute to critical self-talk, poor judgment, or impulsive behavior that gets so many adults in trouble.

Abandonment

Abandonment is a life experience that can resonate for years to come. Infants need both physical and emotional bonding in order to survive, and when, for any reason, these are not available, a memory of unfulfilled needs is created. This is compounded by a belief on the part of the child that they must somehow have done something to deserve being abandoned, or that they somehow are unworthy and unlovable. This sets in motion a potential lifetime of struggling to earn love through caretaking, people-pleasing, over-performing, or any one of a number of ways in which people strive to ensure that they are loveable and won't be abandoned again.

This, of course, directly impacts feeling worthy, and predisposes a person not only to become a perpetual victim, but also to a predilection for addictions as well. Many users find that methamphetamine is particularly effective at soothing those gnawing self-doubts and fears of abandonment and unworthiness. For example, if men have over-invested their self-worth in their physical appearance, they risk crisis as they age and find that their looks are changing. They may not be catching as many eyes, getting cruised as often, and may even begin to feel invisible. The same can be said for men who are long-time survivors with HIV/AIDS. They often experience lower moods, less energy, feeling less attractive, and a general disconnect from the community. These losses trigger old feelings of abandonment and unworthiness, and make them particularly vulnerable to mood-altering chemicals that become a form of self-soothing behavior.

One of the ironies of feeling abandoned is that it becomes a self-fulfilling prophecy. If someone fears being left out or left behind, they may try that much harder to earn acceptance or to fit in. This creates a false self that is ultimately rejected by friends or loved ones if characteristics are developed which cause people to perceive one as too intense or trying too hard. In either case, one's worst fear of being abandoned may become a reality as people become wary of the intensity and erratic behavioral patterns, or the sheer drama that is frequently evident in such relationships.

The issues described thus far—aspects of shame, abuse, and abandonment, and all the resulting beliefs and conclusions we create about ourselves—lead to specific patterns of behavior that further fuel the addictive process, the most well-known of which is so-called codependency.

Adult Patterns that Fuel Addiction

Codependency

In each of the scenarios described at the beginning of this chapter, an effort to escape painful feelings was significantly enhanced or even made possible through the use of methamphetamine. While each of those vignettes was a moment in time, it is possible to identify patterns of escapist thoughts that reveal lifelong patterns of behaviors which make a person vulnerable to addiction and keep the compulsive process alive and rolling forward. Many of these behaviors fall under the rubric of codependency, defined as "continued investment of self-esteem into the effort to control both oneself and others in the face of serious adverse consequences."[3] Trying to claim responsibility for meeting the needs of others often results in the exclusion of one's own needs and boundary distortions around intimacy and separation.

Codependency has been written about extensively, and its causes are well known. Physical abuse (often disguised as "discipline"), sexual abuse, emotional abuse, and intellectual abuse (attacking a child's ideas or opinions, or neglecting to teach a child how to problem solve), as well as spiritual abuse all lead to codependency. As a result of experiencing one or more of these, a child creates a variety of beliefs about him/herself, including an overdeveloped sense of responsibility, an inability to determine what is normal, difficulty having fun or being spontaneous, and tending to lie when it would be just as easy to tell the truth. Codependents also tend to be reactors to situations. All of these set the tone for future addictive behavior in an effort to numb uncomfortable feelings or accentuate other emotions (such as crossing the fine line between fear and excitement and getting involved in excessive risk taking or taboo behaviors). They even result in dissociating into fantasy to totally detach from emotional discomfort.

Boundaries

As we have seen, shame is a learned behavior that is frequently the result of family of origin dysfunction (this can be addiction, mental illness, or any other situation that creates concern in the child that he/she or their family is somehow "different."). Children intuitively understand these secrets. If someone's father is an alcoholic and unpredictable, a child doesn't need to be told not to invite his friends home. He just knows not to do it. Such dysfunction also creates another issue that directly affects future compulsive behaviors: inappropriate boundaries.

Boundaries are those physical and emotional edges by which we define ourselves. All of us need healthy boundaries because they allow us to identify and respect our needs, feelings, opinions, and rights. Healthy boundaries create healthy relationships. By establishing clear boundaries we define ourselves in relation to others. Maintaining good boundaries requires a degree of self-knowledge, otherwise our efforts to create them would be like putting a fence around a yard without knowing the property line.

Boundaries have many characteristics. These may be physical (such as personal space or respect for one's body, including sex) or emotional (being resistant to persons who are overly intrusive and involved). They can be too rigid (such as when someone refuses to allow another person near enough to form an intimate relationship) or too loose (such as when someone becomes too intimate too fast or becomes overly trusting without really knowing a person). Healthy boundaries are firm but flexible, meaning that the person setting them has sufficient self-awareness to respect him/herself while adapting them to certain situations.

As a therapist, I know that maintaining clear boundaries with clients is essential for a healthy therapeutic relationship. Clients are not friends, and a professional sharing too much information creates confusion. There have been occasions, however, where a client is struggling with a particular issue related to living with HIV. In such a case, I may choose to share an example from my own experience that could benefit the client, allowing that boundary to become a little more flexible for a clear therapeutic purpose, without losing recognition of the therapist/client relationship.

Learning to set healthy boundaries is uncomfortable for many people because it may be uncharacteristically assertive. Most of us know when an interaction with someone has slipped into uncomfortable territory. It is good practice to be aware of your feelings and any messages your body is telling you. Red flags may go up when we think: *"why is he telling me all this—it's too much information,"* or *"he doesn't have a right to ask that of me,"* or, *"that friendly hug lasted a little too long."* Sometimes individuals set a boundary accompanied by an apology, or verbalize it indirectly, or never really set it at all. A healthy boundary can be expressed firmly and respectfully, but without apology or rationale. Here are some examples:

- "I'll be happy to drive you to your friend's house as soon as I finish my work."
- "I'd be happy to lend you twenty dollars as soon as you pay me back what you already owe."
- "I'm happy to discuss this matter when you are able to speak calmly about it."

Each of us should expect to have our healthy boundaries challenged—it is up to us to maintain them both for self-respect and our own emotional well-being.

The Victim Triangle

A useful conceptualization of dysfunctional patterns that fuel addiction is the "victim triangle," best described in Diane Zimberoff's book *Breaking Free from the Victim Trap: Reclaiming Your Personal Power.*[4] In this book, Zimberoff describes how a person becomes entangled when moving between several dysfunctional roles in their relationships with others. These roles have their roots in our dysfunctional families of origin, and until someone breaks free of this trap, they are caught up in a repetitive pattern of frustration, emotional pain, and feelings of powerlessness.

Within a dysfunctional family, members caught in the victim trap move easily between one of three roles, and they remain trapped in this triangle until they respond to triggering situations from the position of a strong, responsible adult. Such traps occur in family structures in which an individual experiences a lack of power along with unclear boundaries. The first leg of this triangle is the role of victim. The victim experiences self-pity and shame, and tends to blame others for their woes. He or she feels helpless and is prone to many forms of addictive behaviors. Over time, victims become very creative at constructing situations from which they need to be rescued, and as such often feel frustrated and angry. This anger easily leads them to play the other roles in the triangle (described below), that of rescuer (who constantly steps in to rescue the victim) or persecutor, in which they blame the rescuer (or others) for their victim woes.

The family member acting out the role of helpless victim is supported by the second role in the victim triangle: the rescuer. The rescuer enables the other's behavior and addictions, and experiences feelings of martyrdom while discounting his or her own needs. He uses shame and guilt to control others and avoid his true feelings. As Zimberoff notes, in such a dynamic, love is frequently confused with pity. The relationship between victim and rescuer is characterized by guilt and self-blame. Ironically, the rescuer himself quickly becomes victimized when the victim, who doesn't accept responsibility, blames him. The rescuer is driven by a need to be needed, and is prone to stress-related illnesses and, over time, tends to attract both victims and persecutors.

Completing the third leg of this triangle of roles is the persecutor (who can also become a victim). When a victim lashes out at his rescuer he becomes a persecutor. Another member of the family may also play this role. For example, if a father is angry with a mother for "coddling" her son, he becomes a persecutor for both of them. Despite his anger (or withdrawal), he may also feel victimized by this dynamic. The persecutor expresses rage and blame that becomes abusive toward others. He or she uses shame and guilt to control others and displays emotional and physical withdrawal. He too denies feelings. The relationship between the rescuer and persecutor is one in which guilt and shame are turned into accusations.

Healing the victim triangle takes both awareness and dedication. The patterns cited above are lifelong and deeply ingrained. One must work hard to develop an awareness of feelings and learn how to express them appropriately. Victim patterns need to be shifted from self-pity to self-esteem. Perhaps most important, approval dependent on others must be transformed into approval from within. Rescuers have similar healing tasks that involve releasing responsibility for others and becoming responsible for themselves, including expressing their own needs and feelings. Persecutors must release blame and heal their own shame. The entire system requires clear boundaries and the release of blame, along with extinguishing of addictions.

Discovering Worthiness

Whether playing the role of victim, rescuer, or persecutor, every member of a dysfunctional system feels a "lack of worthiness." I prefer the term "worthiness" to encompass several other commonly used concepts (such as self-esteem) because I feel this is at the core of many of the uncomfortable feelings that undermine one's sense of self and can make a person vulnerable to addictions.

Initially, many people can't see that they have an issue with worthiness, because it operates in subtle ways. Grandiosity is a form of inflated worthiness. An exaggeration of one's talents, capacities, or achievements is really a defense against a disturbing core belief that one does not, in reality, have those qualities at all. Grandiosity can also take the form of diminishing someone else's beliefs, accomplishments, or dreams. It is a hurtful effort to compensate for a perceived imbalance in emotional, intellectual, or physical stature. A feeling of inferiority is really the opposite side of the same coin. If one feels substandard, or second rate, or somehow "less than," this is also usually a way to compensate for unworthiness. People are often surprised to realize that feelings of inferiority and grandiosity are really just different ends of the same continuum.

Another harmful method used to compensate for a sense of wounded worthiness is perfectionism. Experiencing perfectionism means living in a constant state of never being good enough. It fits very well with the victim triangle described above, and indeed is a core dynamic that keeps people trapped within that triangle. Perfectionism derives from early childhood messages that actually rob us of experiencing the benefit of making mistakes. A toddler experiments in the world, trying to stand up, falling, and getting back up again. A child has a marvelous sense of exploration (as long as he can go back frequently and check in with his anchor, usually his mother). Perfectionism destroys one's ability to accept his or her mistakes, to learn from them, and ultimately to become empowered.

Many of my clients have struggled to differentiate between striving for excellence and experiencing perfection. They often become quickly frustrated and give up, repeating to themselves their particular form of self-talk that sustains this perfectionism and their belief that they are unworthy. *"How could I think I could do that? What an idiot!" "You never can do anything right."* The task is to be gentle with oneself. When frustration is experienced it is useful to call upon one's inner strong adult to come forth and comfort that inner child, who is really that part of oneself who is experiencing frustration. Underneath, this inner child is always feeling great fear fueled by the belief that he is somehow unlovable and will be abandoned.

Letting go of perfectionism is not the same as letting go of doing our best and having high expectations. It means letting go of unreasonable and *abusive* expectations of ourselves that we use to perpetuate old emotional pain and keep us locked in the victim triangle.

A disrupted sense of worthiness also produces a powerful force that pulls us out of living in the present into either the past or the future. It is common to go back in our minds to relive events long past or slip into the future to worry or anticipate. When this becomes a preoccupation it is destructive. Many people who have experienced a trauma or some other negative event begin to focus on that incident to the exclusion of their life in the present moment. They ask themselves how that could have happened, or question their actions or reactions, and relive the event emotionally. This is frequently accompanied by the victim mentality described earlier, and as a result, they find it very uncomfortable to stay in the present.

The same force pulls people out of the present and into the future, as well. Fear of what will happen takes the form of "what if" thoughts, which are paralyzing. This is rooted in a sense of powerlessness and/or a lack of responsibility. It quickly blinds someone to their own power and skills. This is not to say that we can influence every life situation or outcome, but we usually have the ability to remain empowered enough to be more proactive rather than reactive to life. There is skill involved in discerning the difference between planning and worry. Worry tends to be a circular form of obsessive thinking in which facts, fears, or scenarios are played out in one's mind, almost always without complete information, and from which few, if any, practical action steps emerge. With planning, on the other hand, one determines what can be influenced and what must be accepted, and acts accordingly. Studies have shown that someone who retains this sense of control is happier and healthier—both physically and emotionally.

Healthy worthiness is the sense that one not only feels good about oneself (based on a combination of self-esteem and competence), but also that one is living up to fundamental human values and living with integrity. This means following through on commitments, one's word, and expressing feelings readily and honestly. The false self, created by a person living with shame, ruptures one's sense of integrity, and of course, worthiness. This must be healed in order to live a sustained recovery. The twelve steps are one important way to rebuild this sense of worthiness and integrity, along with serious psychotherapeutic work on oneself in both group and individual contexts.

Having examined the long arc of the recovery process, as well as the persistent nature of dysfunctional patterns in our lives that perpetuate addiction, we are ready to explore the emotional landscape and its feelings that are inextricably linked to addictive behaviors. Instead of avoiding or numbing emotions, the healing journey requires that we acknowledge and process them.

10

Embracing Feelings

Evan had never been comfortable with his attraction to other men. This discomfort hadn't prevented him from having numerous sexual liaisons, but they almost always took place with the chemical courage found in mood-altering substances. Without their protective shroud he was terrified of both physical and emotional intimacy.

> **Before recovery, when things got too intense I used meth. It's like "I don't give a damn" in drug form.**
>
> — METH USER

When asked about which feelings made him so uncomfortable about expressing his sexual desires, Evan was at a loss for words. He admitted it was now much easier for gay men to be open than before, but despite that freedom, he felt a sense of trepidation about truly expressing his feelings. Evan stated that he sometimes felt unworthy and undeserving, which, in ways that were not even conscious, gnawed at him and subtly undermined his confidence and self-acceptance. This feeling of shame was so deeply ingrained that he, like many, truly believed he *was* flawed. The words "I am damaged goods" resonated with him at a profound level. This feeling of shame, along with a host of other negative emotions, was a co-conspirator in his addictive behavior and had to be addressed in order for him to get clean.

Beyond shame, Evan felt an additional feeling: fear. He believed that if he was truly open about who he was, no one would want him. He felt that his secrets, which before coming out had included his sexual attraction to other men, still held great sway. They included a peculiar sexual fetish, a history of being unfaithful to several partners, and most important, a history of sexual abuse by a cousin that lasted over a period of three years. This ongoing abuse was very confusing for Evan. He was humiliated and shamed by the fact that he had enjoyed the attention and physical pleasure from those encounters. He knew that this sexual contact was wrong, but as a child he had been eager for love and connection. These were all secrets that Evan did not want anyone to know about and that, together, kept him in emotional lockdown.

When he discovered mood-altering drugs Evan believed he finally had a solution. Drugs filled the hole that caused him such pain. Drugs numbed his discomfort with himself, with others, and even with his longing for a spiritual connection. Of all the substances he tried, meth helped him forget his emotional wounds while adding an additional dimension: it fueled fantasies built on his deepest drives that, at least at first, propelled him into wondrous psychological spaces. While he found them to be intense, terrifying, and thrilling, the free fall back to reality was ultimately devastating.

Meth seemed to offer a brief solution to his deep desire for connection that was impeded by layers of shame and false beliefs. Having concluded at a deep level that he was unlikeable and/or unlovable, he created a false self that he presented to the world. This external "shell" was bolstered by hard work, a good income, and hours at the gym (fueled by steroids). Evan made a great presentation to others, but inside he still believed that he was flawed. Because of this belief, he discounted the judgment of people who were attracted to his good looks and charm because he felt those people were drawn to his false external shell, not his true inner self. He later admitted that he believed, "there's got to be something wrong with someone attracted to me" and was dismissive of them. "At that time," he said, "I found healthy people pretty boring."

Longing for connection is a profound and universal human experience. When internal beliefs and their resulting feelings (such as shame) disconnect us from our true selves, a painful void is created. While all addictive behaviors serve to bridge this gap, meth is particularly destructive because it not only numbs that wound, but also creates a world that appears more attractive than reality. Over time this creates significant damage, particularly in the sexual realm. The destructive intensity of meth-sex hijacks desire, leaving little interest in what many meth users see as an uninteresting life of vanilla sex.

Healing sexual desire and learning (often for the first time) to create intimacy are the long-term objectives for recovery from meth. But this requires deeper healing of old, false core beliefs, as well as learning to manage feelings in a healthy way. Without these skills, the longing to numb or escape with drugs will continue to bubble up from deep within, resulting either in relapse or a "white-knuckle" recovery that lacks happiness and a sense of living a fulfilling life. This chapter guides the reader in this process.

Understanding Feelings

Feelings play an essential role in maintaining good physical and mental health. They are not only an awareness of our conscious state of mind, but also of sensations derived from all of our senses, such as touch or smell. For the purposes of this book, I will use the words "feelings" and "emotions" interchangeably. Conscious mental awareness of a feeling is always reflected in a bodily sensation due to the very powerful mind-body connection. Although I use the terms "body" and "mind" separately, I believe they comprise a single entity that is inherently unified.

Feelings are a form of healing for the body as well as the mind. They represent essential feedback that allows us to evaluate our stimuli in our environment, both good and bad. These feelings frequently have a physical manifestation: a yawn, tears, a sigh, or laughter are all expressions of feeling. It is helpful to remember that feelings are an important barometer that guides us in our reactions to what we are experiencing. You don't have to justify your feelings; you have a right to them.

Physical sensations are often the primary "feeling" experience for people who are not accustomed to being in touch with their emotions. My client Drew, for example, always had difficulty expressing anger. In certain triggering situations he was acutely aware of a hot ball in the pit of his stomach, despite his mind remaining seemingly calm. Drew gradually learned that, for him, anger first showed up as a physical sensation. Experiencing that sensation in his stomach helped him realize, "I must be angry." To some people this sounds absurd, but each of us have particular feelings that we find difficult to identify and express. Becoming aware of the physical expression of certain emotions is an important step in managing feelings (as is a *lack* of physical sensation, which may indicate emotional shock).

Core Feelings

Many clients arriving in my office with substance-abuse concerns are confused about what they are feeling. Whether through addiction, loss, physical illness, pain, or depression, their feelings have melded into a ball of discomfort from which they seek relief. It is necessary to help them identify exactly what it is they are experiencing, where they feel it in their bodies, and what events occurred before they felt it. Many therapists utilize handouts with drawings of faces expressing various feelings that can jump-start a person's ability to identify feelings and distinguish them from thoughts. While there are endless shades of various emotions, there are several core feelings that everyone experiences. Negative core emotions include fear, hurt, sadness, grief, guilt, loneliness, and shame. Positive emotions include joy, love, happiness, exuberance, and a sense of inner peace.

It is useful to take a moment and experience your own relationship to each of these feelings. How do you experience fear? Take several deep breaths and recall a recent time when you experienced fear. What is the image that you get when you recall this situation? What is happening in your body when you think about that event? If that sensation were an object, would it be hot or cold, rough or smooth, heavy or light, bright or dark? Adding other dimensions helps people begin to develop a deeper knowledge of their own emotions, as well as more intimate connections with their bodies. Are there other times you have had this same or similar feeling, and if so, what do they have in common? Become aware of any thoughts that are connected with this feeling, including any "self-talk" chatter that may be judging you for this feeling. Finally, consider what you want to do with this fear. Do you have an urge to avoid it, or numb it, or express it in healthy or unhealthy ways? Repeat this process for all the core emotions listed above and develop an awareness of your relationship to each. As you practice this and experience various feelings when they are triggered in your daily life, you may notice that they change and shift. Developing self-awareness about your own emotional patterns is a vital step in the healing process.

Some readers may have noticed that anger was not listed among the core emotions. While anger is certainly a strong and universal feeling, it has a unique relationship to the other core sentiments. Anger is secondary; that is, when one is experiencing anger there is always a feeling lodged deeply underneath it. The real core feeling can be exposed if one drops down under the anger. Hurt often lies at the bottom, but it may include other core emotions as well. People frequently get trapped in anger, the expression of which provides a momentary sense of relief but does not really address the underlying core feeling. If someone drops below the anger, they can experience that deeper emotion, usually hurt, sadness, or fear, and begin to process those feelings and move forward with growth.

Feelings must be identified and expressed in a healthy way. Repressed feelings will cause physical symptoms or illness, as well as emotional complications. Both the mind and body hold memories of feelings that should be released. Reactions to trauma, grief, and anger are commonly retained in muscle memory. It is very common, for example, for someone to begin to sob or experience other strong emotions while receiving some form of body work such as a massage. Western science is only now beginning to quantify the complex ways our bodies and minds process emotions. Repressed anger, for example, may be linked to both a diagnosis of cancer and the speed of its progression.[1] Other studies show that the heart is central to processing emotions. People really can die of a broken heart.[2] Studies have also shown that depression, anxiety, and a lack of connectedness to others are detrimental to heart health.[3,4]

Many people have been taught through negative experiences that their feelings only create problems. Expressing an emotion may have resulted in criticism, shame, or even verbal or physical abuse. As a result, beginning at an early age, children quickly learn to question, hide, or justify their feelings. It's important to remember that feelings don't have to be rationalized or explained.

Avoiding self-judgment of one's feelings is extremely difficult, but it is critically important. If I am feeling shame, it is important to identify it and release it. I don't want to get trapped in a cycle of shame (or any negative feeling). It's important to remember that feelings are feedback. What does this feeling say about me? How does it reflect my beliefs about myself? Is that belief something I have the ability change? There will be more about this important step a bit later. For now it's important to remember that emotions are important guideposts for the healing journey, and need to be observed and acknowledged as they emerge.

Once identified, feelings must be released. There are healthy and unhealthy ways to do this. Repressing feelings (not expressing them at all) leads to a number of complications, including rage, depression, manipulation of others, passive-aggressive behavior, and as noted earlier, stress-related illness. Maladaptive expression of emotions creates emotional, physical, or spiritual abuse of oneself or others. Healthy expression of feelings through direct and assertive expression will lead to better emotional and physical health and a satisfying sense of connection with inner selves and those around us.

Shock

It is not unusual for someone to be unable to identify a feeling at any given time. This happens if people get "triggered," which means that the information or feelings that are currently being experienced activate memories of older, similar situations. At that time, if feelings related to those earlier experiences were avoided by "checking out" or dissociating from them, this will likely happen again. It also occurs if the resulting feelings are too disturbing. In such cases the mind cleverly disconnects from emotions to protect itself from being overwhelmed, just like a fuse. This disconnecting process is called shock, and it may take several forms. While it serves to protect us, it can, over time, result in someone's inability to fully process events and feel their feelings.

Trauma in any form is one example of such an overwhelming event. When someone experiences a traumatic event, it is not uncommon for them to describe leaving their body and observing themselves from a distance, often from above, as in near the ceiling. This reaction is a protective instinct allowing survival in the moment. It does have a long-term impact, however, because certain psychological "pieces" of oneself can be "split off." For example, someone who experienced sexual abuse may have no memory of the event or feel any emotion about it, and they may even be unable to experience intimacy with safe loved ones.

Other traumatic events may not be as catastrophic in the moment, but they still have a powerful impact because they occur over a long period of time. An example of such ongoing trauma might be bullying, which takes a tremendous toll on the individual. Bullying takes away a person's sense of safety or personal power, and deeply wounds a sense of self. Part of the healing work of traditional psychotherapy (and nontraditional forms, such as shamanism) is helping the client retrieve these lost pieces of themselves and reintegrate them, a process sometimes called soul retrieval. This is powerful work that requires expertise and training, but which can result in profound healing for the client.[5]

There are two types of emotional shock that result from an experience of trauma or the triggering of emotions from an old event.[6] The first is called sympathetic shock, which is basically the engagement of the "fight or flight" response. This is full survival mode for the body. Someone in sympathetic shock will be limited in their ability to identify a feeling, but they will notice physical sensations. They may begin to feel hot, or feel their face flush, or get agitated. This can be treated by asking them if they would like an ice pack, by drinking a cool drink of water, or even by moving around physically, all of which helps to get the person back into their body so that they are able to once again begin to feel the disturbing emotion and process it.

A second form of shock is parasympathetic shock, which can be described as the body wanting to shut down and "play dead." People may become very quiet and feel physically cold. When asked, many clients experiencing this form of shock find a warm pad to be soothing, along with a drink of hot liquid such as tea. Deep breathing or physical movement are also helpful to move someone out of both parasympathetic shock.

As people begin to explore feelings and the deeper, personal experiences that relate to them, they will encounter shock. During these moments it is best not to engage the mind by focusing on cognitive questions or other thoughts, but rather to focus on physical sensations, such as asking oneself (or a client) where one might be experiencing a feeling or sensation in the body. Getting in touch with one's body is a grounding experience. When a person is once again able to feel, it becomes possible to move closer to the uncomfortable emotion. This takes time and patience because the conscious mind will try to push the feeling away. With support and guidance, these feelings can be identified, expressed, and released, thereby resolving wounds that keep people trapped in an old emotional space and that provide a fertile ground for addictive cravings.

It should be noted that judgment and sensitivity need to be applied in the expression of feelings. Sometimes people misinterpret the directive to be "totally honest" as permission to say or do things that will hurt other people. In such cases I have found it wise to consult with a trusted advisor. While it is true that expressing an emotion is important, if such expression unnecessarily hurts someone else, or if that person is unavailable or deceased, the better choice may be to release that feeling in a healthy way that does not directly involve the other person. One time-tested example of this is to write a letter expressing hurt, anger, or whatever feeling is causing distress, share the letter with a trusted advisor, and then destroy it. This symbolically releases emotional energy in a way that does not cause further complications. When it is clear that a direct conversation is required, one should convey the message with assertiveness and not with anger or passive-aggressive behavior.

One typical concern of people who have not been in the habit of regularly expressing feelings is a fear that, if opened up, those feelings will never stop and will ultimately overwhelm the person. Tony was a client of mine who lost his partner to AIDS in the late 1990s. At the time he had lost many friends, and the death of his life partner was the ultimate blow. He shut himself off from his emotions and never allowed himself to truly grieve. When he came to therapy he was deeply depressed, had disturbed sleep, and was experiencing respiratory problems. He was using meth and other drugs with increasing frequency in an attempt to numb his pain. He believed that if he allowed himself to open up the deep well of grief inside him, he would never stop crying. He felt he would be engulfed in sadness that would ruin what was left of his life.

Of course, Tony's life had already been hijacked by the unexpressed grief. Blocking those feelings of loss had resulted in cutting off many other feelings as well, including positive emotions. Tony began his healing work by creating safe emotional anchors that would ground him as he began to explore his sadness. These included deep breathing exercises followed by thinking about a "safe place," a soothing spot in his mind where he could retreat momentarily to regain emotional balance. He also consciously fostered an awareness of loving and supportive figures he could "call in" to the sessions. In his case, he was able to recall his maternal grandmother who had been one of the few adults in his childhood who treated him with kindness. A final anchor Tony found useful, despite his anger at God, was a spiritual belief in something greater than himself.

Once Tony had these tools he was able to begin to approach his grief. At first he felt nothing, and stated that the work made him feel "embarrassed and stupid." He had to work to be gentle with himself, but with some patience and persistence he began to really focus on the knot in his stomach. By focusing on the physical symptom he was able to bypass his thoughts, which had been insistent that he avoid feeling these emotions. He focused on that sensation in his stomach, noting its texture, temperature, shape, and color. He was surprised that he began to not feel sadness or grief, but rather anger. He started to feel incredibly angry at God, HIV, and most of all, his partner. "How could you leave me?" he shouted. When he first blurted out these words he was shocked, but with a little coaching and encouragement to yell into a pillow, he was able to keep expressing these feelings. At first the words were rote and disconnected from the emotion, but they gradually became engaged with the old feelings of anger and even betrayal at being abandoned to feel his pain alone. As the anger was expressed, the feeling suddenly shifted, and Tony began to sob. He wailed into the pillow as years of pain finally became unblocked.

This release of feeling was both essential and dramatic. Tony's ability to express his grief required an awareness of physical sensations connected to his feeling, as well as the words to express and move his energy. Once these were engaged, the anger was unblocked and the hurt and pain of his loss bubbled up. After about five or six minutes of sobbing and crying Tony looked up from the pillow. Although his eyes were puffy, his face looked like that of a different person. He looked relieved, relaxed, and even younger. When asked about the pit in his stomach, Tony reported that it was gone.

Tony's work wasn't done, but that therapy session was a pivotal moment in sending him on a journey to heal from the pain of his loss. Contrary to his early concerns, he was not overwhelmed with grief, but actually empowered by the process. He went further by connecting this feeling to his body through breathing exercises, until Tony acquired an even more powerful sense of self-awareness, and, to his astonishment, his asthma symptoms cleared.

Direct expression of emotions in real time is ideal. This simply means that one is aware of physical and emotional events as they occur, and of what is happening to trigger those reactions. It is important to try to avoid judging these feelings. This is, of course, easier said than done. Once noted, they can be expressed or released, thereby avoiding future energetic blockages that cause both emotional and physical problems. If someone practices this process and gains proficiency in it, they will feel more connected, as well as experience more feelings of joy, love, exuberance, peace, and creativity.

Naturally, life offers more than wonderful, "feel-good" emotions. We cannot exist in a constant state of love, joy, and exuberance. If we are open to life and connected to others, there will be periods of pain and sadness. The key is that we don't have to become mired in those feelings. Expressing them is a process for which there is no correct plan. Healing old wounds is not a linear process, but rather an organic one, moving from one phase to another and then perhaps back again. I believe that if we identify and express uncomfortable feelings as they occur, we can maintain a state of living in positive energy and feelings. When we are engaged in the energetic flow of life it feels good. Our creative spirit and our connectedness fuels a healthy balance in our physical and emotional lives.

The Danger of Boredom

One specific emotional state needs to be mentioned because of its central role in healing from addictions: boredom. Many people are surprised at the power of boredom in their relapse behaviors. This makes sense if one thinks about the amount of time demanded by an addictive behavior. It involves the ritual of anticipation; acquiring the drug and/or creating the situation (people, places, things), acting out, and recovery time. This entire process can occupy days, and when that addictive cycle is removed from someone's life, they find that they have too much unscheduled time on their hands.

For someone recovering from addictive behavior, such unplanned time is a dangerous thing. Cravings and fantasies pop up with great frequency, and boredom provides an empty stage on which they begin performing tricks for the mind. It is essential to have strategies to combat boredom. This may be as simple as scheduling one's time with recovery-based activities so there are no large gaps of time in which they have no plan. It also means acquiring new habits and hobbies that begin to replace those empty hours with productive endeavors. Because so many people who have addictions find that they frequently feel isolated, a great rule of thumb is to fill free time with activities that connect them to other healthy people and supportive environments. These may be meetings, volunteer work, or attendance at other various support groups.

Self-Talk

One of the most annoying and common concerns which frequently interferes with feelings is what is called "self-talk," the chatter in our own heads that is often judgmental and even cruel. This talk typically echoes old messages received at an earlier age, which were internalized at a deep level and now serve only to limit the ability to break free of various situations that hold people back, including addictions.

In his excellent workbook on anxiety, Bourne[7] outlines four major varieties of self-talk. The first of these is "the worrier," which promotes anxiety. Such worrier talk would typically begin with statements like, "what if..." Examples might be, "What if I embarrass myself?" "What if I make a mistake?" or, "What if I lose control?" The worrier is proficient at creating fears of the worst case scenario, and will catastrophize any situation, often leaving the person stuck in a state of fear. When listening to the worrier, a person seems to be abandoned by many of their adult skills, regressing back to an early period when they may indeed have been helpless. In such cases it is useful to turn down the volume of the worrying chatter and remind yourself of the skills you possess, which you can apply on your own behalf should things turn sour. Hopefully the worst-case scenario will not happen, but it is sometimes useful to go through a mental rehearsal of how you would react in order to reconnect with an awareness of your adult tools and skills.

A second category of self-talk outlined by Bourne is "the critic," whose voice will say things that promote low self-esteem, such as, "That was stupid!" or, "Can't you ever get this right?" or, "Why are you always this way?" This voice is one of constant judgment and negative evaluation of one's own behavior, incessantly pointing out one's flaws and limitations. If the critic is prominent among your voices, it is useful to examine how you compare yourself to others and take special note of what positive qualities about yourself you tend to ignore. It is also helpful to observe if there are any "weaknesses" or qualities that you are particularly sensitive about. Where do those perceptions come from, and how reality-based are they?

A third category of self-talk is "the victim," which promotes feelings of helplessness and hopelessness, and frequently results in depression. The voice of the victim frequently speaks the words, "I can't," or, "I'll never be able to, so what's the point of trying?" or, "Maybe I could have done it before but it's too late now." The victim frequently evolves from a feeling of shame and believes that he or she is flawed, defective, or unworthy. These are old, taught beliefs that can be unlearned and replaced with new, more accurate beliefs. If you frequently feel victimized, it's useful to hear the specific words you use to voice regrets, complaints, or deficits. How true are they? What really are your options? What other blocks may be preventing you from experiencing positive feelings and real satisfaction? It is also helpful to review the information on the victim triangle presented earlier in this book.

Bourne's fourth category of negative self-talk is "the perfectionist," a pervasive and destructive voice that promotes chronic stress with the words, "I should," "I have to," or, "I must." This voice is closely related to the critic, but the perfectionist's voice drives one to become more ambitious and try harder, while the critic seeks to undermine one's self worth. If perfectionism is a problem, it's useful to make a list of your personal "shoulds," including not only things you need to accomplish, but aspects of your own character that you find particularly intolerable. It's also important to identify how you may use external sources to bolster your self-worth. As noted by Downs in *The Velvet Rage*, these include occupation, money, status, people-pleasing, and many more.

Changing Negative Self-Talk

There has been a vast amount of research addressing how to change negative self-talk, most of which can be classified into a broad modality called cognitive behavioral therapy (CBT). The first wave, or precursor to CBT, came from behavioral psychologists such as Skinner, whose work postulated a theory of learning in which all behaviors were said to be acquired through conditioning, a process whereby behavior is influenced and modified by consequences.

A second wave occurred with a focus on the cognitive processes themselves. The work of such important figures as Albert Ellis[8] and Aaron Beck[9] led to formal techniques designated as cognitive behavioral therapy (CBT). Rather than addressing the traditional focus of so-called psychodynamic therapy, such as developmental issues stemming from childhood experiences and dream interpretation, CBT addresses problematic beliefs that lead to troubling feelings or behaviors.

Events (A) + Interpretive Thoughts (B) = Feelings (C)

The model for cognitive behavioral therapy is best described by imagining that our thoughts serve as intermediaries between events in the world (A) and the feelings directly resulting from those events (C). CBT reminds us that "thoughts are not facts" and "I am not my thoughts." By changing the thoughts (B) that interpret or intervene on our perception of events (A) around us, we can influence the feelings (C) we experience as a result of those experiences. My client José, for example, was very hurt when an old childhood friend named George failed to return his call. José had always looked up to George, who, among all his high school friends, had reached the highest levels of the corporate world. By all external accounts George was very successful. José, on the other hand, had struggled with his sexual identity and dropped out of community college to care for an elderly parent. José believed that he would never be as successful as George and experienced a consistent chatter in his head that told him he wasn't good enough and would never amount to anything.

When George didn't return his call, José felt crushed. He realized that he had invested a portion of his self-esteem in his relationship with George, and now felt that this childhood bond had been broken. He felt angry and hurt that his old friend couldn't be bothered to return the call. The critic in his head came alive, and he berated himself. These feelings quickly led him to feel victimized by George's callous failure to contact him.

Using CBT, José discovered that he had some control over the hurt and angry feelings he experienced from this incident. He began to separate himself from the critical voice in his head, realizing it didn't necessarily speak the truth. He learned to interrupt those negative statements and replace them with positive, more affirming ones. "I am a caring friend," and "I am worthy," were substituted in the tug-of-war in his head. With practice, José began to realize that his false belief of unworthiness was creating the hurt and angry emotions he felt, and was reinforcing his self-criticism and low sense of self-esteem.

José felt very empowered by the practice of cognitive behavioral therapy and began to see all kinds of opportunities to apply these principles in his life. Ironically, George did call José after about two weeks. After much apologizing, George told José that he had been in South America dealing with his father's medical emergency. His silence had nothing at all to do with José. This allowed him to uncover another dysfunctional pattern in his thoughts: jumping to conclusions.

A third wave of CBT has emerged, which incorporates the concept of mindfulness.[10] Building on the traditional model described above, aspects of mindfulness simply add a dimension of paying attention to the present moment with intention and without judgment. The goal is to interrupt automatic thoughts that result in a persistence of negative feelings, including depression. Mindfulness skills emphasize developing an awareness of those automatic processes and avoiding reacting to them. Instead, one is encouraged to observe the automatic thoughts without judgment and alter one's reaction to the stimuli.

Techniques of mindfulness-based CBT include observing, describing, acting with awareness, and extending non-judgment. Where traditional CBT can be summarized as, "catch it, check it, and change it," mindfulness-based cognitive behavioral therapy (MBCBT) says, "catch it, observe it, and let it be." A typical MBCBT strategy would be to induce relaxation with deep breathing and/or some other technique, develop an awareness of the "here and now," expand that into a broader awareness, include the observing self, and incorporate non-judgment, acceptance, and compassion. Finally, one would identify and practice alternative reactions to the triggering incident.

Utilizing Our Emotions

Many books could be written (and have been!) about improving one's ability to manage feelings, both in terms of addiction and in general. As recovery takes root, the numbing, boosting through fantasy, or even the soothing comfort created by the insulating effects of substance use and addictive behavior fade away. Emotions, both good and bad, begin to emerge and feel overwhelming to someone who has not experienced them directly for years. A lifetime of accumulated feelings begins to bubble up into consciousness and must be managed. Many people discover that even activities that should be pleasant are so over-stimulating that they become uncomfortable and threatening. This is particularly true for sex and intimacy, which many gay men have rarely experienced without the protective insulation of mood-altering chemicals.

In early recovery, the world seems very intense. It is easy to find another way to soothe oneself by transferring addictions. By applying the tools described in earlier chapters, as well as the techniques to manage feelings described here, the benefits of recovery and sobriety itself begin to blossom. Old beliefs about ourselves that resulted in all kinds of negative feelings can be rewritten. With intention and patience, we reinvent ourselves.

It is important to remember this is not a linear process of addressing old wounds or pivotal experiences on a one-time basis. These old experiences will emerge in many ways and forms, but a portion of healing takes place each time we identify, feel, and release those emotions. The next chapter examines seven essential skills that make healing and growth both an exciting and rewarding journey.

11

Seven Essential Tools for a Strong Recovery

Sustained and meaningful recovery from any addictive substance or behavior requires numerous skills, some of which are quite natural and others that require both willingness and effort. In some cases, mastering these tools or concepts make the healing process more comfortable or meaningful. A solid and true recovery involves not only physical liberation from the addictive process, but emotional and spiritual restructuring as well. Longstanding feelings will feel extremely raw once the substances or processes are taken away. We come face-to-face with what have been rightly called "old demons," which may be of our own making or may have been imposed upon us. No matter the source, it becomes our task to sort through them in order to move our lives forward. This process requires a set of skills that provide the support we need to address the emotional backlog created by a lifetime of addictive or pre-addictive behavior.

> **Everything without crystal, including sex, is so much more intimate and meaningful. That's both the scary part and the reward of recovery.**
>
> — METH USER

1. Cultivating Mindfulness

Mindfulness is sometimes poorly understood and, in my opinion, often viewed as an overly complex process. For Buddhists, mindfulness is one of the seven essential factors leading to enlightenment: gaining insight into the workings of our mind, which trap us in craving and suffering. The concept is similarly used in Hinduism, and relates to liberation from the cycle of death and rebirth. In the west, we have recently engaged the concept of mindfulness as a valuable tool that increases our awareness of the world around us and, most importantly, the world within us.

Mindfulness can be described as an attentive awareness to the reality of things or simply "what is." As odd as it sounds, most people trudge through their days without really being mindfully engaged. They operate on "automatic pilot," moving from home to work or school, interacting with colleagues or friends, and end up back home again, often without cultivating an awareness of what is really happening both internally and externally as they move through these motions. They may experience a sense of dread when they first awake, or have a slight headache. It's all too common to take some kind of medication or have an extra coffee to numb the physical symptoms before moving on. They may encounter someone in the course of their day who triggers an unexpected reaction.

Why is she looking at me that way?
I have a bad feeling about him.
I don't like how she treats her child.
I've got to get out of here.
Why is my foot so jittery in this meeting?

Uncomfortable feelings may accumulate to the point where they break through into awareness, and all too often they are dispatched with medication, drugs, or some other diversion to nullify them.

For the purposes of this book, mindfulness is nothing more than cultivating a conscious awareness of what is going on around us and our reactions to it. Our physical and emotional experiences constantly give us clues about our feelings and their meaning. The long downward spiral of addictions often reduces this conscious awareness to a point where people react only to the most basic and obvious emotions, usually fear. Many addicted persons lose the ability to identify what they are feeling or what they want.

With mindfulness, we are reinstalling a few more gauges and indicators on our control panel. Ironically, they are already present; we simply have to start paying attention to them. We must also be alert to overloading our ability to handle information. We need to pay attention but not to be so hypervigilant (overly sensitive to what is going on around us) that we, in essence, become emotionally paralyzed. With time and practice it becomes possible to become much more aware of thoughts and feelings, to trust one's intuition, and to become aware, in real time, of how we are reacting to people, places, and things. This knowledge is an important guide in helping us identify the things we need to work on in order to consolidate our recovery.

I think of mindfulness as an activity that occurs only in the present tense, and can be incorporated in many ways. Some people like to listen to music, really focusing on the rhythms, the vibrations, or the variety of sounds. Other people practice various forms of meditation, which includes rhythmic breathing. Focusing on one's breath is a powerful way to become mindful as well as experience all its benefits, including a reduction in stress and an increase in levels of self-awareness. Someone also may find that a walk in nature where they really focus on the shapes of leaves or the sounds of birds grounds them once more in a heightened level of awareness.

Techniques of mindfulness are limited only by creativity. I have clients who practice mindfulness while gardening and connecting with the earth, while stroking their dog or cat, or even while doing tasks such as housework that might, by some, be considered anything but soothing. I have had the experience of increased mindfulness while painting a room. There is something about the task itself, the visible evidence of progress, and the rhythmic nature of the brush strokes that makes this a pleasant task.

The human brain requires engagement to stay vital and alert. Mindfulness is a way to keep the brain interested and increase our awareness of what's happening inside us so that we may react accordingly. A repetitive activity that causes our brains to go into an automatic mode increases our risk of being overtaken by uncomfortable feelings, cravings, and even acting out. Try driving a different route on your daily routine or eating a new type of food. Challenging oneself (within reason, of course) is a good thing. That is not to say that some daily practices, particularly in how you begin and end the day, aren't important. I feel that while maintaining such brief routines are both grounding and essential to stay in balance, over the arc of our lives it is essential to have variety.

Mindfulness becomes a powerful tool to combat cravings and to begin to rewire some of the associations between drugs and other behaviors, particularly the fusion of meth and sex. Cravings for either sex or drugs are usually the only conscious part of a much larger system of associations beneath the surface. Often tied to emotions, these connections are usually rooted in the uncomfortable or unpleasant feelings we want to avoid. We have learned that drugs help us control these feelings through avoidance, numbing, or in some cases, even escalation (such as thrill seeking and danger). After a period of time we are aware only of the craving and begin to lose touch with the initial spark of feeling that set it off. Mindfulness is the key to regaining this important insight.

2. Embracing Self-Compassion and Forgiveness

Patience with oneself, as well as others, is a critical skill that carries enormous power to pull one through the sometimes choppy waters of recovery. Once it becomes clear that a behavior or set of behaviors has become personally destructive, and once one has accepted that change is necessary, it seems progress cannot be made fast enough or complete enough. A significant amount of frustration is generated by our own impatience and judgment toward ourselves and those around us, attitudes that are often based on flawed or unrealistic expectations.

When I introduce the concept of patience to clients in early recovery, they often object by saying they simply don't have time for it. Most people think of patience as a characteristic of persons (or higher beings) with a good deal more strength than someone who is dealing with the accumulated destruction that comes with active addiction. Of course, people often have pressing issues such as legal or medical concerns that require immediate attention. We have to triage our own lives and take care of things requiring intervention. It is not unusual for someone in early recovery (or beyond) to be completely overwhelmed by the problems they face and to literally not know where to start. In such cases, assistance may be required by professionals, sponsors, friends, and family to break tasks down into smaller, "bite-sized" pieces—a process called partializing.

I consider patience not only just a matter of endurance in the face of uncomfortable feelings and events, but also an attitude that confers kindness and gentleness upon ourselves. The changes that are necessary for sustained recovery and growth require time and effort to take root and grow. Many relapses have occurred because people became impatient with the pace of their recovery, took shortcuts, or decided to ignore the wisdom around them. Patience, to me, is the ability to persevere calmly through both good times and bad. It means being gentle with ourselves when old thoughts and even old behaviors arise. It means calling on our inner wise adult to regain emotional balance and not to feed frustration.

Patience in today's world seems like a rather antiquated concept. Most of us have become accustomed to life with "the cloud," where our e-mails, contacts, appointments, and other artifacts of our daily lives are instantly available. I can recall a sense of increasing agitation when an appointment I entered on my smart phone took a few minutes to appear on my desktop. As a society we have become dependent on a constant feed of information, a process that actually runs counter to what I believe are healthy habits for recovery. It is healthy to be able to regularly drop off the grid in order to take stock of our inner lives. In a sense, this constant reliance on external devices further disconnects us from our emotions, thoughts, and even intuition. Some forward-thinking companies have begun to realize that twenty-four hour availability actually reduces productivity, and are requiring employees to turn off their phones when not at work.

Methamphetamine, in particular, lends itself to impatience. I recall many clients in my office with tapping feet, unable to sit still, describing feelings of emotional jitteriness, and trying to keep up with their minds, which were racing from one topic to the next. All of this led to a mounting sense of anxiety and dread. It is indeed difficult in such circumstances to remind oneself to be calm and accept changes that occur at what seems like a geologically slow pace of recovery. This is particularly true when there are so many consequences and crises that inevitably follow in the wake of meth and other drug use. The recovering person has to develop strong skills to force him/herself to slow down. Focusing on self-compassion, along with the other skills mentioned in this chapter, is useful to break the cycle of anxiety (and ultimately panic) that demands relief in the form of a drug or some other compulsive behavior such as overeating or overspending.

One of the major complications of becoming kinder and gentler with oneself is perfectionism, a habit that is longstanding for most people, and especially for addicts. Perfectionism is defined as excessively high performance standards for both oneself and others, accompanied by a short-fused intolerance for anything that falls short. It becomes a vicious cycle, where nothing is happening quickly enough or at high enough standards, and which leads to a supercritical response whereby negative self-talk and angry outbursts at others takes place. This, in turn, often sparks remorse, leading to even more critical self-talk and striving for perfectionism in interpersonal relations. The byproduct of these tornadic emotional cycles is any number of negative feelings, all of which ignite the urge for the drug of choice or an addictive process to numb them.

Perfectionism usually has deep roots in one's parental relationships. Whether conscious or not, our behaviors and the need to please and to do everything "perfectly" has been linked to love and acceptance. At some level, at least in the child's eyes, being perfect feels like a matter of life or death. We fear abandonment (or sometimes anger and rage) if we don't do things perfectly. As adults, the conscious sources for these deep lessons have often dropped below the surface, but they operate silently and efficiently in our subconscious, driving our behaviors with predictable and sometimes bewildering precision.

Changing perfectionism requires focusing the basis of our self-esteem and love to a more reliable source—namely away from external people or behaviors to ourselves. Becoming aware of self-talk, as described earlier, is half the battle. Once we identify this constant chatter, we have the choice to turn down the volume or, more ideally, stop it altogether. We can consciously correct those old, incorrect thoughts and assumptions, and begin to have some control over our emotions by changing the intervening thoughts and assumptions that control them. Only by turning down this constant internal source or agitation are we able to begin to find some sense of inner peace and self-acceptance. This is a long process that takes committed practice. Most of us have carried these internal critical voices with us for years, and they are deeply ingrained. This is where patience and the need to root out perfectionism go hand-in-hand.

Some people in recovery misinterpret (or manipulate) the concept of being imperfect. *Does this implicitly give me permission to use? How does accepting imperfection affect my recovery?* I believe we owe it to our integrity to avoid playing games with drug use or to utilize concepts such as patience and perfectionism to rationalize relapsing into old behaviors. Should relapse happen (and with meth it almost always does before a firm recovery takes root), it is important to stop the drug use as quickly as possible. Many people tell themselves that since they have already relapsed, they might as well ride the elevator all the way to the bottom. *"I'll keep using drugs since I've lost my sobriety anyway."* This is a dangerous strategy because, as any drug user will admit, outcomes are unpredictable when one cedes control over to the use of drugs.

Self-care also complicates being patient with oneself. Specifically, this is related to the sometimes conflicting concepts of self-nurturing versus self-indulgence. For many, taking care of themselves somehow feels like a selfish act, nearly an act of betrayal. Self-nurturing, the behavior we are striving for, should be viewed as a necessity that involves soothing our emotions and physical bodies. It isn't a luxury, but rather an essential and important aspect of being healthy. It takes many forms, including a healthy diet, adequate rest, taking time for ourselves, speaking our feelings, and not being overly hard on ourselves.

For individuals who have long focused on taking care of other people's feelings or needs (and not their own), this can feel like self-indulgence. This undesirable behavior is characterized by attempting to correct negative feelings (such as being depressed, feeling empty, or overwhelmed) with the use of a shortcut, be it drugs, addictive behaviors, or simply trying to escape or numb the feeling. Whether it is overeating, running up a credit card for a four hundred dollar pair of shoes (the "high" from which will be short-lived), or "letting someone have it," it is a failing strategy with the goal of soothing ourselves and sedating bad feelings. Discerning the difference between self-nurturing and self-indulgence is a critical skill for recovery.

3. Connecting with Your Inner Child

Many people of a certain age approach the idea of the inner child with skepticism, often rooted in *Saturday Night Live's* Stuart Smalley, and his affirmations to himself and his inner child. While entertaining, these sketches had the regrettable consequence of making the concepts humorous and even a little ridiculous. This is indeed unfortunate, because the inner child is tremendously valuable and lends insight into feelings and behaviors, as well as serving as a reliable tool for discerning feelings or motivations.

The inner child is that part of us—all of us—that is the sum of experiences from birth through a time before puberty. It lies largely below our conscious thoughts. The concept goes by various names. Carl Jung is thought to have originated the idea, which he called the "Divine Child." Other writers have ascribed different names: Emmet Fox called it, "Wonder Child;" Charles Whitfield called it the, "child within;" and perhaps best known, at least concerning addictions, is John Bradshaw's, "inner child," which he described as an accumulation of unresolved childhood conflicts and ongoing childhood dysfunction.

I think of the inner child as holding a collection of raw feelings, which, as experienced by a young child without an adult's perspective, remain puzzling, hurtful, and in some cases, charged with the urgency of life or death. For example, a child may experience being left behind (once or multiple times), which may create an inner child that holds a lingering sense of abandonment. Lacking reason, the child may conclude that they are somehow unlovable and unable to attract or keep someone who will love him or her. The child may conclude (consciously or not) that, in order to survive, they will have to make some behavioral adaptations. These may involve withdrawing to avoid feeling dependent on anyone, or over performing to guarantee that someone will be there to provide love and support.

The inner child, then, is the young child within us who continues to re-experience our adult interactions through the eyes of a child. This is most obvious when someone "triggers us." Perhaps we take offense at the behavior of a colleague who never says anything positive about our work. This may bother us more than we are able to explain. In fact, that person may elicit an angry reaction within us that is far out of proportion to the actual encounters. When such reactions occur, our inner child has been triggered, and is reacting with pure feelings. In this case, that feeling may be fear that resonates with a childhood experience regarding caregivers who were always highly critical.

A small child has no choice but to believe that criticism directed at him/her by an adult is the truth. They simply don't have the neurological wiring to refute or challenge such criticism. As adults, we have acquired this verbal ability but, by then, the feelings of the inner child are deep-set and subconscious. At a conscious level we may not be aware of what is driving a feeling of fear, dread, or even anger.

Why is this important for recovery and healthy living? The impulse to use substances and other addictive behaviors is often driven by negative feelings experienced by the inner child. For example, if one's inner child is feeling fear, they may not be directly aware of this emotion but rather experience a sudden craving for their drug of choice. If the inner child is feeling lonely, they may have an impulse to act out in an unhealthy way to soothe that empty feeling.

In the book *Taming Your Outer Child*,[1] Susan Anderson elaborates on this concept by adding a third component, the "outer child." She describes the outer child as that part of ourselves who acts out the unexpressed feelings of the inner child. It is the outer child that embraces addictive behaviors in an attempt to sooth the unresolved feelings of the inner child. It is the outer child, then, that personifies the addictive impulse fed by a need to soothe, numb, or escape the discomfort that the inner child doesn't know how to handle.

The solution, according to Anderson, is to utilize our healthy adult self to manage both our inner and outer children. The healthy adult is the wise part of us that has learned that feelings are necessary, and that we deserve safety and security, and are most certainly worthy of being loved. Healing requires getting in touch with that strong adult within us to acknowledge and reassure our inner children with all the tools of a wise parent. If our inner child is experiencing terror and our outer child is expressing that feeling through bad behavior, we need our healthy adult to step up and set boundaries, lovingly reassure, and remind all parts of ourselves that things are not out of control. Both the inner and outer child need reassurance by the wise adult within us to say that we are safe and loved and things will be okay.

Such internal reassurance very often feels unnatural because we have frequently become accustomed to berating or criticizing ourselves (and our inner child) for being scared or feeling lonely, or in some cases, feeling any emotions at all. Learning to recognize what is going on inside and to react gently and with wisdom is an essential skill to self-soothe, and therefore to maintain and sustain recovery.

4. Discovering Your Shadows

Most of us have had the experience of walking into a room, meeting someone, and having an instant attraction or dislike to them. We may have been puzzled by this, since we had never met or even heard about the person. It may be something about their tone of voice, their body language, or even their clothing. The strength of these feelings can be quite extreme, which is equally puzzling. What we may be experiencing at that moment is a glimpse of one of our "shadows."

Jung first described the "shadow" or "shadow aspects" as unconscious elements of our personality that are unrecognized by our conscious awareness. These are often parts of ourselves that we dislike or would find extremely distasteful were we to admit that we have them. While usually negative, there are positive aspects of the self that remain beyond the reach of conscious recognition as well, such as a personal strength that for whatever reason is unacknowledged by an individual.

Typically, however, shadows remain the domain of unattractive characteristics, thoughts, or feelings that we would rather not acknowledge in ourselves. These aspects are prone to projection; that is, rather than see that we possess these traits, we note them in other people and are easily triggered by them. That is why we can have strong reactions toward someone we have never met before. If our unconscious self recognizes one of our shadow elements in that person, our conscious mind rejects any identification with them and projects very negative feelings onto the person exhibiting the characteristic. This creates a great opportunity to explore our own shadows, which typically remain elusive. Uncovering them may be a struggle since the conscious mind fights identifying with these negative characteristics.

Shadows are elusive. For example, a person might judge people who are too loud and aggressive in social situations. This may actually stem from a discomfort with speaking up and asserting oneself. The self-doubt of the person making those judgments gets projected in the form of passing judgment onto those who have no such problem, because of their own shadows.

It has become practically a cliché to point out that many individuals who make the most ferocious anti-gay pronouncements and devote great energy to introducing anti-gay legislation or creating reparation therapy programs to "cure" homosexuality are themselves struggling with shadows. These men may not be aware of their own deep, unconscious feelings, at least initially. If shadows are at work, they may only be aware of their revulsion about homosexuality, which was in fact strong negative feelings (even hate) projected onto homosexuals in order to deny their own internal impulses. The conscious mind defends itself against these feelings and often fuels aggressive opposite actions, such as an anti-gay agenda, which can be destructive.

It is important to remember that all of us have shadows that need to be better understood in order to live more consciously and avoid sudden roadblocks thrown up by our unconscious minds. Once we start to become conscious of those parts of ourselves that we would rather disown, we begin to move toward a healthier integration of all aspects of ourselves. Such assimilation of these unwanted parts of ourselves is an ongoing process because our awareness deepens with more recovery.

Shadows fuel addictions for several reasons. They cause extreme psychological discomfort that the conscious mind desperately desires to suppress or numb. Compulsive behaviors effectively distract the mind from this unease while causing all kinds of other complications. As in the cases mentioned earlier, someone may be struggling with strong same-sex attraction, but be unable to admit it to themselves (or later, to others). Alcohol and opiates temporarily numb these feelings and force those unwanted parts of the self to remain in the subconscious. Someone else may be struggling with unexpressed anger. In such cases, their shadow is demanding to be recognized while consciously abhorring people expressing that trait. The disinhibiting effect of drugs such as alcohol and amphetamines allow these feelings to be expressed, sometimes with the excuse that the substance itself was the real culprit responsible for any negative behaviors.

Methamphetamine has been used by gay men consistently to enhance sexual experiences. While it is obvious that meth use leads to terrible consequences, many men describe the drug's effectiveness at allowing them to express themselves sexually without concern or inhibition. They describe this initial experience as very liberating. One man stated, "On meth I could finally celebrate gay sex and being gay." This disinhibition, of course, results in a lack of concern about precautions for safer sex or, for that matter, about one's sexual partner.

Meth also allows deep and dark parts of ourselves to rise to the surface and become sexualized. I have had many clients who describe increasingly dark and violent sexual fantasies on meth. Once in recovery, they are very disturbed and even traumatized that such dark scenarios could arise from within their own minds. While it is difficult to discern the role of the drug as creator or disinhibitor of such fantasies, it is certainly worth examining them through the lens of shadows. *What dark feelings are bubbling up that need to be identified and appropriately released?* There are abundant opportunities to learn a little more about one's darker urges and to begin the work of assimilating them into our conscious awareness.

Acknowledging our shadows is vital to a meaningful and sustained recovery. It is the shadow parts of ourselves that fuel negative self-beliefs or provide a seemingly logical rationale for ongoing compulsive thoughts or actions. Shadows provide a mechanism through which our higher self remains locked in place, unable to grow and progress into higher levels of conscious living. I think of shadows as tethers connecting us to invisible parts of ourselves. They have been attached for so long it is easy to forget they are there, yet if they become activated, they give us clues about feelings and urges that are just beyond our conscious awareness.

The amount of energy required to keep our shadows in place is significant. In her book, *The Dark Side of the Light Chasers*,[2] Debbie Ford describes this effort as akin to trying to hold a big beach ball under water. It requires concentration and physical energy, usually to no avail. Once we reclaim shadows as our own, a tremendous amount of energy is released that we can use for other purposes.

In many ways, shadow work fits nicely with the twelve-steps because they both share the goal of acceptance of self. Through the process of a fourth step inventory and fifth step disclosure, as well as taking ownership of our behavior and the making of amends, profound healing takes place. Both step work and shadow work stimulate great resistance, including those times when we are simply unable to see ourselves as clearly as others see us. At such moments we simply have to be open and allow the people with whom we interact to mirror back to us aspects that we need to accept about ourselves. This work leads to self-acceptance and, ultimately, a great deal of personal power. As Debbie Ford states, "the very impulses we most fear may be the key to what is lacking in our lives."

5. Fueling Optimism

Everyone has heard the expression, "is the glass half empty or half full?" Scientists have discovered that we are born with an innate optimism about the world,[3] and that negative assumptions are actually learned thought patterns. More and more medical studies are showing that people with positive attitudes have better health outcomes, and a healthier life may translate into a longer one. In a study conducted by the Albert Einstein College of Medicine's Institute for Aging Research,[4] researchers found that people lived longer if they had a positive attitude toward life, characterized by being optimistic, easygoing, extraverted, laughing more, and expressing emotions rather than bottling them up.

I recall my client Sam, who one day arrived at my office angry and upset that a total stranger had approached him while he was shopping for groceries and said, "Smile, it can't be that bad!" "Can you believe that?" he asked, before adding, "And that's not the first time that's happened." He was embarrassed that his mood was painfully obvious to everyone he encountered, yet he was defiant at his right not to mask his feelings from anyone.

In session, we processed Sam's justifiable upset at the presumptuous stranger who intrusively offered him good-natured feedback. Sam was dealing with some serious physical issues unknown to anyone but his closest friends and family. He felt outraged that anyone would judge him without knowing all the stressors he battled on a daily basis. It was easy for him to focus on the inappropriate actions of this stranger, but then our conversation came back around to his second comment, that this had happened before.

Sam admitted that he was angry and tired after years of juggling meth addiction, HIV medications, physical concerns, and more losses than he could enumerate. He viewed the world skeptically, and he didn't dare take the chance of investing too much emotional energy in being hopeful. He found some paradoxical comfort in cynicism, which, while often painful, allowed him to move through the world bolstered against disappointments. He had survived a great deal and felt no need to force himself into pleasantries that seemed unnatural. This stranger's remark, however, struck a nerve, and was the tipping point in Sam's recognition that he retained some power over choosing positive or negative feelings as he maneuvered through the world.

Sam had long understood that there is a link between attitude and physical health. He knew, for example, of the placebo effect, in which the power of the mind influences physical changes in ways that remain a mystery, yet he was skeptical of the power of a positive attitude with respect to overwhelming physical problems. He had always been, appropriately, wary of oversimplifying this approach into a belief that could, essentially, "blame the victim." That is, a belief which held that those who become and remain ill somehow have flawed attitudes and beliefs about themselves. Now, however, it occurred to him that while positive thinking might not hold magical curative powers, it certainly could improve his ability to live with his illness, which, in turn, could indeed have health benefits. He began to realize that his negative outlook had slowly evolved without any conscious thought.

That day, and in subsequent sessions, we processed Sam's skill in identifying and expressing his feelings. He began to understand that challenges and even tragedies occur in everyone's lives, and that the significance of these events lies in how we frame them and make sense of them. He reacted defensively at first, dismissing a positive attitude as a simplistic form of denial. But Sam gradually began to see shades of subtlety in this approach. He identified a deep-seated fear that if he were to accept that parts of life are truly beautiful, it would somehow negate the terrible things he had experienced along with his pain and struggles. Sam realized he could honor his grief and anger (and perhaps begin to process them) and still find room for positive and hopeful thoughts. He exhaled deeply when he realized he could begin to redefine his worldview.

Over the course of several months Sam found one exercise particularly helpful in refocusing his attitude toward greater optimism. He became aware of "self-talk," the constant (usually critical) chatter inside our heads described earlier. He began to hear the pessimism of this inner voice, and once aware of it he gained some expertise in tuning it out. He discovered that this chatter rationalized his negativity by saying, "it's just the way I am." He began to see that this wasn't necessarily true and that he had the power to choose alternative attitudes. For example, if he told himself, "there's no way this will work," he tried to put a positive spin on it by saying, "I can try and make it work." Or, if his inner voice said, "this is too complicated," he revised it by thinking, "I'll try it from a different angle."

Optimism slowly crept into Sam's life in a way that took him by surprise. Of course, he still had bad days filled with fear and anger and sadness, but on most of those days he also experienced hints of gratitude and even happiness. After some months he noted with a sly smile that it had been a long time since a total stranger asked him what could be so terribly wrong.

We are flooded every day with massive amounts of data that our brains struggle to process. Over time, our brains develop shorthand methods to pick out which of the many bits of information we should notice and, if appropriate, take action to address. Eventually we begin to notice only the negative things happening around us and not see the positive aspects. With conscious effort and some heightened awareness this can be changed. Like Sam, we can urge ourselves to become at least a little more realistic in noticing the good and the bad. Such a balanced approach will impact our daily functioning, our ability to remain clean and sober, and the quality of our lives.

6. Practicing Gratitude

My client Sam, who struggled with embracing optimism, struggled with another concept essential to a robust recovery: gratitude. For Sam, this initially took the form of a gratitude list. Sam rolled his eyes when it was suggested that each morning he create a list of ten things for which he was grateful. He reluctantly tried it, and soon discovered that this simple practice had great power. At first he struggled to identify even five such things, but he eventually acquired the habit of observation and began to naturally notice both his positive and negative experiences and interactions.

Feeling grateful does not come naturally to many people, especially LGBT persons. Years of negative reactions, bullying, stigma, and high rates of addiction and mental health problems are certainly a legitimate cause for worry and concern. Even the times when most people give at least a fleeting acknowledgement to gratitude, the holidays—especially Thanksgiving—are often difficult, and for good reason. Money problems may seem overwhelming, and emotional stress may result when our friends, and sometimes even our partners, aren't welcomed by our families of origin.

So how can we achieve an attitude of gratitude, or should we, as one client of mine pointed out, "save it for the greeting card companies?" Gratitude, the practice of being grateful, is increasingly being recognized as a powerful tool that actually changes our outlook and moods.

I know from personal experience that there is nothing harder than being grateful when things are difficult. Whether due to personal illness, a major loss, or even worry generated by watching too much cable news, the idea of having gratitude when you are experiencing pain or fear seems ludicrous, if not offensive. I have had many clients stare at me in disbelief when, during an emotionally or physically painful period, I suggest they try finding a few things for which they might be grateful.

Most simply ask, "Why?" The reason is because it not only makes you feel better, it may even change the world (more on that below). The shift in personal consciousness created by the act of identifying gratitude moves us from a state of need and resistance to one of acceptance and healing. I recognize this is sometimes easier said than done. In recent years I experienced sadness and pain around the declining health of a parent. I certainly wasn't grateful for that situation, but even on the worst days it was possible to appreciate a ground orchid in my yard, or my dog's relentless playfulness, or the steady support of my partner. Taking a few minutes to consciously acknowledge those things somehow broke a spell and brought me back into balance.

While many spiritual traditions have long recognized the wisdom of gratitude, its power is now being increasingly documented in scientific literature. For example, one study by Emmons and McCullough in the *Journal of Personality and Social Psychology*[5] used a double-blind study to demonstrate that a conscious focus on one's blessings has empirical emotional and interpersonal benefits. Many other studies link gratitude with numerous positive effects, ranging from well-being to goal attainment.

Even if being grateful helps us feel better, can our personal expression of gratitude have an impact on the world? Increasingly, many people think so. A number of metaphysical traditions (as well as quantum physics) acknowledge the power of our thoughts to change our very cells, and even our reality. Today there is a heightened awareness about the potential of shifting human consciousness based on what we as individuals think about and what we do.

The Internet is increasingly being used to facilitate such shifts. I recently learned of one free site (www.gogratitude.com) that is attempting to create a wave of gratitude which will sweep the globe. One can subscribe to receive brief daily messages that help develop such awareness. To date, over one million people have signed on.

Recovery, health, and life itself are challenging, but even the worst situations can be improved by focusing on gratitude. When it seems most difficult the universe will often remind us, whether in the form of an unexpected phone call from a friend or your dog arriving with a toy, of opportunities for gratitude.

7. Developing Empathy

Healing for both individuals and communities rests on the practice of empathy by all concerned. Empathy is a frequently misunderstood term. It is defined as "the ability to see things from another person's perspective, to understand that person's feelings, and convey that understanding back to the other person." Deceptively simple, the ability to emotionally connect with and support another person, and to feel what they are experiencing, requires self-awareness.

As the brain becomes better understood, scientists are learning a great deal about empathy. They have found that empathy allows a person to imagine—in very real, emotional terms—what another person is experiencing and to feel it along with them. There is no doubt that such an ability gave humans an evolutionary advantage. Whether empathy is innate or learned is not known, although most scientists have long considered humans to be born with the capacity, noting that infants seem to connect with and share rewards with others.

It is clear from scientific and anecdotal evidence that methamphetamine decreases the ability of a person to have empathy. This can be seen in any number of examples, from the very high rate of child abuse among meth-using parents to hard-core sex acts that objectify, sometimes with brutality, one's sexual partners. Part of recovery from meth, then, involves reexamining one's ability to have empathy. A level of acceptance and forgiveness for oneself is an essential beginning for rebuilding any empathic skills that may have been eroded by meth use.

Empathy is generally understood to have three components: recognizing feelings in others, learning to listen, and letting others know you understand. It may seem that recognizing feelings in others is not a difficult task, but studies of meth users have documented that this is, indeed, a problem. In this research,[6] men using meth were shown photographs of faces clearly displaying various feelings such as anger, happiness, and sadness. The men using meth consistently performed more poorly at identifying these emotional expressions, most often reading anger or some other hostile feelings into the faces they observed. This is consistent with the suspicion and outright paranoia that develops with ongoing use of amphetamines. Recognizing the feelings of others, then, may require some extra work for meth users.

The second important step in practicing empathy is learning to listen. Again, this sounds simpler than it is. One must put aside distractions that interrupt the interchange of communication. Distractions also convey to the speaker that they aren't important or that attention is not being paid fully to them. The introduction of mobile phones into nearly every social situation dramatically complicates our ability to avoid distractions. How many times have you been in an important conversation when a notification alerts you (or the other person) that a new message has arrived or a phone call has been missed? This breaks the energetic flow between individuals in a way that is harmful to the focus of the discussion and to developing empathy itself. Finally, minimizing any interruption is important. If you need to have an important conversation with someone, it is useful to first inquire if it is a good time or, if not, when it could be scheduled.

The third and final step in empathy is letting others know you understand. This involves mirroring back to your partner (simply repeating what you just heard them say) as well as asking for more detail. It also includes letting them know that you are able to see how they would feel and, ultimately, that you understand their feeling. Harville Hendrix, founder of Imago couples therapy,[7] has developed a couples' dialogue process that is extremely useful for any conversation between two people. While such communication techniques seem uncomplicated and straightforward, they become quickly complicated with the addition of emotions, reactions, or other strong feelings that undermine their effectiveness and any chance of empathy.

There are a few other considerations in an empathic conversation. One is to be careful not to offer advice unless asked. Many people simply want an opportunity to be heard, which is itself therapeutic. Many of us feel obliged to provide solutions that often disconnect us from the speaker as we begin to problem-solve in our head, even while the other person is still speaking. If solicited, it is of course helpful to provide feedback, but generally one should avoid too much sharing of your own experience. Someone seeking a conversation about an important topic probably doesn't want it hijacked by making the discussion all about you.

We all can feel an authentic connection in our gut. Experiment with this feeling, begin to better understand your own defenses, and practice putting yourself in the other person's place. Those connections—sometimes seen, but almost always felt—are a vital source of healing.

EPILOGUE

Changing the Conversation about Gay Men's Health

As gay men face the challenges of methamphetamine and other drugs, it is important to broaden the scope of discussion to a larger view of gay men's health. In many ways, chronic meth use is just a means to numb uncomfortable feelings or alleviate boredom. As HIV ravaged the community, the positive views of gay men that grew out of gay liberation and Stonewall began to fade into history. The heroism of gay men and lesbians caring for those stricken with AIDS before any other funding was forthcoming was being forgotten. Yet despite waves of challenges, including shame, stigma, HIV, substance use, and even violence, the LGBT community has continued its healing process, building on inherent strengths.

> **It's not really about meth... it's all about reclaiming whatever parts of ourselves we've hidden away or lost as gay men.**
>
> — METH USER

The Gay Men's Health Movement, a national effort driven by gay men and their supporters, is striving to change this pathology dominated approach and, in its place, recognize the many positive qualities and assets that gay men bring to themselves, their friends, and their communities. Gay liberation owes much to feminists who blazed trails in promoting health, self-acceptance, and self-concept among women. In the 1970s and early 1980s, gay men began to reinvent themselves by declaring their right to express themselves emotionally, sexually, and even physically in ways that were natural, but long considered unacceptable.

It requires a shift in the way we think about ourselves. It requires that we ask ourselves to be clear on the facts about gay men, for it is certain that sensationalism often dominates, including in discussions of methamphetamine. We have to heighten our awareness of how we speak about gay men and their issues and the words we use to describe them. We need to ask what conspires to keep us focused on the "deficits" of gay men, and we need to force ourselves to rethink the very real problems in the gay community in order to utilize strategies that rely on the assets of gay men.

Do gay men have problems? Of course, but we systematically minimize the many strengths that gay men have, and have had, for generations. Eric Rofes, in an important article in *White Crane Journal*,[1] describes the history of the Gay Men's Health Movement, which represents a cultural shift about how gay men think about themselves. These changes are being explored at dozens of conferences around the US and the world, and through programs designed by gay men for gay men, all of which begin with the basic assumption that gay men are healthy and happy.

The three general principles of the Gay Men's Health Movement are:

1. Gay men, at root, are individually and collectively healthy, reasonable, life-affirming, and successful in creating fulfilling and meaningful lives.
2. They take an asset-based approach to gay men's communities, rather than a deficit-based approach; they look at and build on inherent community strengths, resources, skills, and values that demonstrate gay men's commitment to survive and thrive even under formidable circumstances.
3. They view gay men as people who share a baseline commitment to self-care, community-care, and disease prevention. They believe that a small group of gay men who appear unreasonable and destructive to themselves are taken as representing all gay men. At

> the same time, they refuse to separate themselves and their movement from these men or write them off as flawed or inhuman.

In addition to the core values expressed above, the Gay Men's Health Movement has recognized that gay men are creative, strong, and resilient—adept at thinking outside the box, taking responsibility, and caring for themselves and others. They know how to get what they want, and they know how to create lives that are satisfying and fulfilling. They've developed their own home-grown social networks, support structures, and communal rituals. Gay men know how to find community—even when it's hidden—and build community, even in the face of formidable obstacles.

Meth and other drug use is seen as yet another layer of stigma that gay men are reluctant to discuss. Finding a voice and the willingness to talk about meth is a challenge for many in the gay community. There is concern of a backlash against what is perceived as irresponsible behavior that could result in more restrictive laws and reduced funding for HIV services and prevention.

All addictive behaviors thrive in secrecy. We need to talk about meth, other problematic drug use, as well as the sociological and psychological factors that play a role in their appeal. Most important, we need to extract morality from our discussions and find real solutions building on the inherent strengths found in the gay community. Only by recognizing and building upon their many strengths will gay men be able to reduce the burden of stigma and shame that create ample opportunities for numbing and psychological escape, and form the social connections that can heal individuals, the community, and the greater society.

APPENDIX

Other Substances Frequently Used with Methamphetamine

Pushing and Pulling Moods

Cocaine, both in powder and crack form, has been consistently used since the early twentieth century, and most recently had a wave of popularity in the 1980s. Cocaine, like methamphetamine, is an amphetamine that produces similar stimulating effects. Cocaine's high is of much shorter duration, however, and as we have seen, it does not release as much dopamine as meth. Another major difference between the two drugs is that cocaine is derived from natural sources, the coca plant, and cocaine molecules wash away from the receptor site. Meth is a synthetic drug with a relatively large molecule that sits on the receptors for a longer period of time, resulting not only in a longer period of intoxication, but also more toxic effects to nerve cells. Meth molecules ultimately pass through the body and are expelled in the urine, a fact not lost on meth cookers who, when desperate for precursor materials, will sometimes recycle the molecules from their urine.

Another amphetamine sometimes used with meth is MDMA (methylene-dioxy-methamphetamine), a psychoactive drug chemically similar to methamphetamine and mescaline. MDMA is also known as ecstasy, sometimes abbreviated by users as "X" or "XTC." MDMA acts on the neurotransmitter serotonin, which affects tactile sensations as well as distortions in time and perception, and is used for mood enhancement as well as to help people sustain dancing. The effects of "X," which increases a sense of empathy and connectedness, are qualitatively very different from meth. Meth, for example, can produce strong feelings of aggression, the polar opposite of empathy. The effects of MDMA are mellower than those of meth, although hostility is associated with both drugs.[1] Mollies, increasingly popular pills reputed to be pure ecstasy, often, when tested, contain methamphetamine or a significantly adulterated form of ecstasy.

As with meth, high doses of MDMA result in a spike in core body temperature that can result in death. MDMA also produces an increase in heart rate and blood pressure that is harmful and may lead to long-lasting physical damage. Confusion, depression, and craving are among the psychological effects of MDMA. Recently in Fort Lauderdale, there were narcotics seizures of methamphetamine that was packaged to look like MDMA, perhaps an ominous hint at a possible strategy to expand demand for meth among ecstasy users. Adulterants in MDMA are common and represent a major risk to the user.

"G" (GHB or gamma hydroxybutyric acid) is a synthetic, central nervous system depressant first used as an anesthetic in the 1960s, and is probably the drug most commonly used with methamphetamine. It was available in health food stores as a bodybuilding enhancer until 1990, when it was banned by the Food and Drug Administration. It produces euphoric and hallucinogenic states in the user, and sometimes renders the user helpless with little to no memory of the time period in which it was used. This has resulted in "G" being used, along with Rohypnol, as a date rape drug. "G" is a liquid that must be mixed with water, which is often done "on the fly" in dance clubs, and frequently results in improper dosing that produces a coma-like state requiring hospitalization, or even causes death.

"K" (ketamine) is another drug that was quite common until law enforcement efforts such as Project TKO by the Food and Drug Administration in 2006 curtailed supply and reduced its availability. Ketamine is used as an anesthetic in human and veterinary medicine, and produces psychotic effects and hallucinations. Its hallucinogenic effects are only visible at lower doses when other sensory stimuli are minimized, such as in a dark room. This contributes to the drug's popularity in dance clubs. "K" can also induce a dissociative state, in which a person feels detached from their body, or it can create distorted physical sensations such as being touched, pulled, or even flying. There are a number of negative respiratory and neurological side effects that are produced by ketamine, especially in combination with other drugs.

Marijuana (or cannabis) is a commonly found drug known for its psychoactive properties and its effects on both mental and physical faculties. There are extensive debates about the dangers of this drug as well as its criminalization, although most professionals agree it is harmful to the brains of developing adolescents. It creates an intoxication very different from methamphetamine, whose users regularly cite this drug as one that consistently mellows the sharp effects of meth, and one that helps maintain a moderately altered state between major methamphetamine runs.

Poppers have been used by gay men for years to enhance sex. This street name refers to various alkyl nitrites (most commonly amyl nitrite and butyl nitrite) which are inhaled and affect the smooth muscles of the body, including the sphincter muscles of the anus. The drug also works on blood vessels in that they relax and cause a sharp drop in blood pressure. Because of this, using poppers with blood pressure medication is extremely dangerous. Amyl nitrite has long been used to treat angina and is a component in products such as room deodorizers and video head cleaners. Because poppers for human consumption are illegal without a prescription, they are sold as video head cleaners in paraphernalia shops, despite the fact that very few people continue to use video tape players.

The head rush associated with the drop in blood pressure is said to increase sexual pleasure and desire at the same time the anus (or the vagina in women) is relaxed. Many men believe poppers prolong orgasm. In combination with methamphetamine, poppers significantly increase the risk of acquiring HIV, as found in a study reported in the *Journal of Acquired Immune Deficiency Syndromes* in 2007.[2] Researchers reported that 93 percent of meth users who also used poppers had a threefold increase in the risk of acquiring HIV, underscoring the synergistic impact of multiple drugs used together.

What Goes Up Must Come Down

Days of sleepless, adrenalin-driven behavior inevitably results in frayed nerves, a depletion of any emotional resilience, and a weakened ability to tolerate stress. At such moments many users of methamphetamine rely on benzodiazepines to calm themselves as their bodies and brains attempt to recover from the drug.

Benzodiazepines are the most widely prescribed central nervous system drug in the United States, although many of the men using them with meth may not obtain them through a prescription. In high doses these drugs act as hypnotics, in medium doses they reduce anxiety, and at low doses they sedate and induce sleep. Common examples of these drugs include alprazolam (Xanax), temazepam (Restoril), lorazepam (Ativan), diazepam (Valium) and clonazepam (Klonopin). They are highly addictive and require a medically-supervised detoxification.

Because methamphetamine constricts blood vessels, which in turn impairs a man's ability to obtain an erection, many men utilize erectile dysfunction drugs to compensate for drug-induced impotence. Drugs such as sildenafil citrate (*Viagra*), tadalafil (*Cialis*), vardenafil hydrochloride (*Levitra*), as well as alprostadil (*Caverject, MUSE*: Medicated Urethral System for Erection) and others that are inserted or injected into the penis, are commonly used by men driven by sexual desire yet unable to perform. In one study,[3] users combining meth and sildenafil were six and a half times more likely to report having had condomless, insertive anal intercourse, significantly increasing the risk of transmitting HIV. There is also increasing evidence that erectile dysfunction has its origin in the brain, where sexual desire has been damaged by overstimulation of drugs and pornography.

One's chances of acquiring other sexually transmitted infections are increased when meth and erectile dysfunction drugs are combined. But there are even greater risks. Meth increases the heart rate and raises core body temperature, while erectile dysfunction drugs dilate blood vessels. The result of this pushing and pulling is that it puts a significant strain on one's heart, increasing the risk of a heart attack or stroke.

Some meth users report they do not enjoy the effects of alcohol. The feelings experienced when drinking are very different from those of meth. Many meth users abhor the sluggish, foggy, sloppiness of drunkenness, preferring instead to experience what they perceive as meth's benefits of high energy, clarity of thought, and broadened insight. While these perceptions are not borne out by actual scientific measurement, meth users often prefer drugs that complement meth as opposed to alcohol that, as one man wrote, "brings me crashing down—when I want that I'll grab a Valium."

Some men firmly believe that alcohol consumption is totally unrelated to meth use, and this belief often interferes with recovery. Many men who never had a problem with alcohol have been brought to their knees by methamphetamine. Once in recovery they believed that, since alcohol had not been a problem, they could drink safely while avoiding methamphetamine. Though firmly committed to giving up meth, some still seek the effect of several drinks, as well as the bar atmosphere so significant in gay social life. This has proven risky for many. Alcohol reduces inhibitions and impairs one's ability to resist the temptation of other drugs. This is especially true when the drinking occurs in a gay bar where the atmosphere of men, cruising, and sex bring cravings for methamphetamine to life. The experience of thousands has shown that abstinence from all mood-changing chemicals, including alcohol, is essential for a stable recovery.

Nicotine is the final drug worthy of mention in the context of methamphetamine. Many men who use meth also use nicotine and continue to do so after giving up other drugs. This drug complicates recovery because, like meth, it has a powerful effect on the reward center of the brain. In 2002,[4] researchers reported that nicotine is the perfect drug for addiction because only a few exposures create a lasting memory of its rewards in the brain. Nicotine, like meth, triggers a release of dopamine, causing pleasurable feelings. Even though nicotine triggers the release of dopamine for only a brief moment, the levels of dopamine in the brain remain high for much longer. Why this occurs was solved by research related to the interaction of nicotine with another neurotransmitter, GABA. Due to this interaction, the "reward" of nicotine continues to be experienced by the user for up to sixty minutes, long after the nicotine levels in the blood have dropped, setting the stage for the use of a highly addictive drug and ongoing cravings.

Continuing to stimulate the reward center of the brain with nicotine at the same time that one is trying to eliminate cravings for methamphetamine and other drugs reduces the chance of quitting any of them. It has been said that nicotine primes the brain for addiction in that it quickly teaches the brain how to become addicted, and maintains the addictive process of craving and satisfaction. This, at least indirectly, has implications for the overall comfort of anyone trying to extricate methamphetamine from their life.

Notes

Chapter 1: Gay Men, Meth, and Sex

1. Paul, J.P., R. Stall, and K. Bloomfield. "Gay and Alcoholic: Epidemiologic and Clinical Issues." *Alcohol Health and Research World* (Spring, 1991).
2. Stall, R., and J. Wiley. "A Comparison of Alcohol and Drug Use Patterns of Homosexual and Heterosexual Men: The San Francisco Men's Health Study." *Drug and Alcohol Dependence* (October 1988), 22(1): 63–73.
3. Marshal, M.P., M.S. Friedman, R. Stall, and A.L. Thompson. "Individual Trajectories of Substance Use in Lesbian, Gay and Bisexual Youth and Heterosexual Youth." *Addiction* (June 2009), 104(6): 974–81.
4. Wong, C.F., M.D. Kipke, and G. Weiss. "Risk Factors for Alcohol Use, Frequent Use, and Binge Drinking among Young Men Who Have Sex with Men." *Addictive Behavior* (August 2008), 33(8): 1012–1020.
5. Friedman, M.S., M.P. Marshal, R. Stall, J. Cheong, and E.R. Wright. "Gay-Related Development, Early Abuse and Adult Health Outcomes among Gay Males." *AIDS Behavior* (November 2008),12(6): 891–902.
6. Ibanez, G.E., D.W. Purcell, R. Stall, J.T. Parsons, and C.A. Gomez. "Sexual Risk, Substance Use, and Psychological Distress in HIV-Positive Gay and Bisexual Men Who also Inject Drugs." *AIDS* (April 2005), 19 Suppl 1: S49–55.

Chapter 2: The Hijacking of Sexual Desire

1. Fiorino, D., and A. Phillips. "Facilitation of Sexual Behavior and Enhanced Dopamine Efflux in the Nucleus Accumbens of Male Rats after D-amphetamine-induced Behavioral Sensitization." *Journal of Neuroscience* (January 1999), 19(1), 456–63.
2. Carboni, E., A. Imperato, L. Perezanni, and G. Chiara Di. "Amphetamine, Cocaine, Phencyclidine and Nomifensine Increase Extracellular Dopamine Concentrations Preferentially in the Nucleus Accumbens of Freely Moving Rats." *Neuroscience* (1989), 28(3), 653–61.
3. "Methamphetamine Use and HIV Risk Behaviors among Heterosexual Men." *MMWR* (March 2006), 55(10).

4. For more information on this see: Tennov, D. *Love and Limerence: The Experience of Being in Love* (Chelsea, Michigan: Scarborough House, 1979).
5. Morin, J. *The Erotic Mind: Unlocking the Inner Sources of Sexual Passion and Fulfillment* (New York: Harper Collins, 1995).
6. Morin (1995), p. 194.
7. Grant, J., and M. Potenza. "Sexual Orientation of Men with Pathological Gambling: Prevalence and Comorbidity in a Treatment-Seeking Sample." *Comprehensive Psychiatry* (November 2006, Epub April 2006), 47(6):515–8.
8. For example, Colfax, G., G. Mansergh, and R. Guzman, et al. "Drug Use and Sexual Risk Behavior among Gay and Bisexual Men Who attend Circuit Parties: A Venue-Based Comparison." *Journal of Acquired Immune Deficiency Syndrome* (October 2001), 28(4), 373–9.
9. Halkitis, P., J. Parsons, and M. Stirrat. "A Double Epidemic: Crystal Methamphetamine Drug is in Relation to HIV Transmission among Gay Men." *Journal of Homosexuality* (July 2001), 41(2), 17–35.
10. Carnes, P. *Out of the Shadows: Understanding Sexual Addiction.* (New York: Bantam, 1983).
11. For example: Mansergh, G., and R. Shoush, et al. "Methamphetamine and Sildenafil (Viagra) Use are Linked to Unprotected Receptive and Insertive Anal Sex, Respectively, in a Sample of Men Who Have Sex with Men." *Sexually Transmitted Infections* (April 2006), 82(2),131–4.
12. Plankey, M., and D. Ostrow, et al. "The Relationship Between Methamphetamine and Popper Use with HIV Seroconversion in the Multicenter AIDS Cohort Study." *Journal of Acquired Immune Deficiency Syndrome* (March 2007).

Chapter 3: The Chase for Intensity

1. Apter, Michael J. *The Dangerous Edge: The Psychology of Excitement* (New York: The Free Press, 1992).
2. Volkow, N., et al. "Evaluating Dopamine Reward Pathway in ADHD." *JAMA* (September 2009) 302(10): 1084–1091. doi: 10.1001/jama.2009.1308. PMCID: PMC2958516. NIHMSID: NIHMS238262. Evaluating Dopamine Reward Pathway in ADHD
3. These are a few of many publications by P. Carnes: *Don't Call It Love: Recovery from Sexual Addiction* (New York: Bantam Books, 1991); *Out of the Shadows* (Center City, Minnesota: Hazelden, 1992); *A Gentle Path Through the Twelve Steps* (Center City, Minnesota: Hazelden, 1993).
4. Carnes, P. "The Obsessive Shadow: Profiles in Sexual Addiction." *Professional Counselor* (1998), 13(1), 15–17, 40–41.
5. Michael, R.T. "The National Health and Social Life Survey: Public Health Findings and their Implications." *To Improve Health and Healthcare 1997* (Princeton, New Jersey: Robert Wood Johnson Foundation, 1997).

6. Schwartz, M.F., and W.H. Masters. "Integration of Trauma-Based, Cognitive, Behavioral, System and Addiction Approaches for Treatment of Hypersexual Pair-Bonding Disorder." *Sexual Addiction & Compulsivity: The Journal of Treatment and Prevention* (1994), 1:57–76.
7. Adams, K.M., and D.W. Robinson. "Shame Reduction, Affect Regulation, and Sexual Boundary Development: Essential Building Blocks in Sexual Addiction Treatment." *Clinical Management of Sex Addiction* (New York: Brunner-Routledge, 2002).
8. Simon, S., et al. "Cognitive Performance of Current Methamphetamine and Cocaine Abusers." *Journal of Addictive Disease* (2002), 21(1): 61–74.
9. Weinstein, S. "Nightlife Suffers as Gay Men Move Online." *The Village Voice.* http://www.villagevoice.com/2012-06-20/news/Nightlife-Suffers-as-Gay-Men-Move-Online/.
10. Gorski, T. *The Gorski-CENAPS Model for Recovery and Relapse Prevention* (Independence, MO: Herald House/Independent Press, 2007).

Chapter 4: Men, Drugs, and a Deadly Virus

1. Washington Post/Kaiser Family Foundation. *Survey of Americans on HIV/AIDS* (2012). http://www.kff.org/kaiserpolls/upload/8334-F.pdf.
2. Halkitis, P., and M. Shrem. "Psychological Differences Between Binge and Chronic Methamphetamine Using Gay and Bisexual Men." *Addictive Behaviors* (March 2006), 31,3 549–552.
3. Zinberg, N. *Drug, Set, and Setting: The Basis for Controlled Intoxicant Use* (New Haven, Connecticut: Yale University Press, 2005).
4. Reback, C.J. *The Social Construction of a Gay Drug: Methamphetamine Use among Gay and Bisexual Males in Los Angeles* (1997). Available at: http://www.uclaisap.org/documents/final-report.
5. Shoptaw, S., and C.J. Reback. "Associations Between Methamphetamine Use and HIV Infection in Men Who Have Sex with Men: A Model for Guiding Public Policy." *Journal of Urban Health* (2006), 2006:83:1151–1157. doi:10.1007/s11524-006-9119-5.
6. Robinson. L., and H. Rempel. "Methamphetamine Use and HIV Symptom Self-Management." *Journal of the Association of Nurses in AIDS Care* (Sep–Oct 2006), 17(5):7–14.
7. Reback, C.J., S. Larkins, and S. Shoptaw. "Methamphetamine Abuse as a Barrier to HIV Medication Adherence Among Gay and Bisexual Men." *AIDS Care* (2003), 15 (6), 775–785.
8. Ellis, J., M. Childers, and M. Chember, et al. "Increased Human Immunodeficiency Virus Loads in Active Methamphetamine Users are Explained by Reduced Effectiveness of Antiretroviral Therapy." *Journal of Infectious Diseases* (2003), 2003:188: 1820–1826.
9. Op.cit.

10. Halkitis, P.N., J.T. Parsons, and M. Stirrat. "A Double Epidemic: Crystal Methamphetamine Drug Use in Relation to HIV Transmission Among Gay Men." *Journal of Homosexuality* (2001), 2001;41:17–35.
11. Op. cit.
12. Mansergh, G., R.L. Shouse, and G. Marks, et al. "Crystal Use, Viagra Use, and Specific Sexual Risk Behaviors of Men Who Have Sex with Men (MSM) During a Recent Anal Sex Encounter." Abstract D04B. National STD Prevention Conference (Philadelphia, Pennsylvania: March 2004).
13. Wong, W., J. Chaw, and C. Kent, et al. "Oral Session CO2B: Risk Factors for Early Syphilis Among Men Who Have Sex with Men Seen in an STD Clinic." (San Francisco: 2002–2003). 2004 National STD Prevention Conference [Abstract on the Internet, cited 2005 April 28]. Available from http://www.cdc.gov/std/2004STDConf/C-OralSympWorkAbstracts.htm.
14. Mitchell, S.J., W. Wong, and C.K. Kent, et al. "Oral Session DO4C: Methamphetamine Use, Sexual Behavior, and Sexually Transmitted Diseases Among Men Who Have Sex with Men Seen in an STD Clinic." (San Francisco: 2002–2004.) 2004 National STD Prevention Conference [Abstract on the Internet, cited 2005 April 28]. Available from http://www.cdc.gov/std/2004STDConf/D-OralSympWorkAbstracts.htm

Chapter 5: Sexual Templates, Themes, and Shadows

1. Kinsey, A., M. Pomeroy, and C. Martin. *Sexual Behavior in the Human Male* (Philadelphia: W.B. Saunders and Co., 1948).
2. Kinsey, A., M. Pomeroy, C. Martin, and P. Gebhard. *Sexual Behavior in the Human Female* (Philadelphia; W.B. Saunders and Co., 1953).
3. Masters, W., and V. Johnson. *Human Sexual Response* (New York: Bantam Books, 1966).
4. Masters, W., and V. Johnson. *Human Sexual Inadequacy* (New York: Bantam Books, 1970).
5. Stoller, R. *Observing the Erotic Imagination* (New Haven, Connecticut: Yale University Press, 1985).
6. Bader, M. *Arousal: The Secret Logic of Sexual Fantasies* (New York: St. Martin's Press, 2002).
7. Money, J. *Lovemaps* (New York: Irvington Publishers, 1986).
8. Money, J. *Gay, Straight, and In-Between* (New York: Oxford University Press, 1988).
9. Money, J. *Lovemaps: Clinical Concepts of Sexual/Erotic Health and Pathology, Paraphilia, and Gender Transposition in Childhood, Adolescence, and Maturity* (Buffalo, New York: Prometheus Books, 1993).
10. Simon, W. and J. Gagnon. *Sexual Conduct: The Social Sources of Human Sexuality* (Chicago: Aldine, 1973).
11. Morin, J. (1995), p. 140.

12. Morin, J. (1995), p. 140.
13. Tripp, C. *The Homosexual Matrix* (New York: New American Library, 1975).
14. Morin, J. (1995), p. 204.
15. Morin, J. (1995), p. 204.
16. Morin, J. (1995), p. 221.

Chapter 6: The Aphrodisiac Effect of Secret Desires

1. Morin, J. *The Erotic Mind: Unlocking the Inner Source of Sexual Passion and Fulfillment* (New York: HarperCollins, 1995).
2. Morin, J. (1995), p. 92.
3. Interesting, methamphetamine (and cocaine) are "visual drugs," meaning that visual processes are enhanced as new neural pathways link the sensation of the drug and vision together. This was evident but poorly understood in the 1980s when I worked in inpatient drug rehabilitation centers. We would show instructional videos that depicted drug use, drug paraphernalia, and actual injecting. Without intending to do so, we had triggered the patients who began to sweat, get agitated, and in some cases, had to leave the room.
4. Morin, J. (1995), p. 94.
5. Hendrix, H. *Getting the Love You Want: A Guide for Couples* (New York: Henry Holt, 1988).
6. Morin, J. (1995), p. 103.
7. Kettelhack, G. *Dancing around the Volcano: Freeing our Erotic Lives: Decoding the Enigma of Gay Men and Sex* (New York: Three Rivers Press, 1996).

Chapter 7: Sex and the Plastic Brain

1. Hilton, D., and C. Watts. "Pornography Addiction: A Neuroscience Perspective." *Surgical Neurology International* (2001), 2011; 2: 19. Published online Feb 21, 2011. doi: 10.4103/2152-7806.76977
2. www.bodywisdomvideos.com
3. Goldstein, I. *The Central Mechanisms of Sexual Function* (Boston University School of Medicine, 2003). http://www.bumc.bu.edu/sexualmedicine/publications/the-central-mechanisms-of-sexual-function
4. Nestler, E. "Brain Plasticity and Drug Addiction." Presentation at "Reprogramming the Human Brain Conference, Center for Brain Health." (University of Texas at Dallas, 2011).
5. Doidge, N., op.cit. 107.

Chapter 8: The Recovery Process

1. Rawson, R., and S. Shoptaw, et al. "An Intensive Outpatient Approach for Cocaine Abuse: The Matrix Model." *Journal of Substance Abuse Treatment* (1995), 12 (2), 117–127.

2. Merzenich, M., et al. "Representational Plasticity Underlying Learning: Contributions to the Origins and Expressions of Neurobehavioral Disabilities." *Perception, Memory, and Emotion: Frontiers in Neuroscience* (Oxford: Elsevier Science, 1996).
3. Doidge, N., et al. 123.
4. Byl, N., S. Nagarajan, and L. McKenzie. "Effect of Sensory Discrimination Training on Structure and Function in Patients with Focal Hand Dystonia: A Case Series." *Archives of Physical Medicine and Rehabilitation* (2003), 84(10); 1505–14.
5. Op. cit. 123

Chapter 9: Healing Old Wounds

1. Nemeroff, C., and M. Hoyt, et al. "The Cognitive Escape Scale: Measuring HIV-Related Thought Avoidance." *AIDS Behav* (2008), 12(2):305–20. doi: 10.1007/s10461-007-9345-1. Epub Jan 11 2008.
2. Downs, A. *The Velvet Rage: Overcoming the Pain of Growing Up Gay in a Straight Man's World* (Boston, Massachusetts: Da Capo Press, 2012).
3. "Diagnosing Codependence." (Issaquah, Washington: The Wellness Institute).
4. Zimberoff, D. *Breaking Free from the Victim Trap: Reclaiming Your Personal Power* (Issaquah, Washington: Wellness Press, 1989).

Chapter 10: Embracing Feelings

1. Thomas, S.P., et al. "Anger and Cancer: An Analysis of the Linkages." *Cancer Nursing* (October 2000), 23:5, 344–9.
2. Wittstein, I.S. "Stress Cardiomyopathy: A Syndrome of Catecholamine-Mediated Myocardial Stunning?" *Cellular Molecular Neurobiology* (July 2012), 32(5):847–57. doi: 10.1007/s10571-012-9804-8.
3. Ornish, D. *Love and Survival: 8 Pathways to Intimacy and Health* (New York: HarperCollins, 1998).
4. Burg, M.M., et al. "The 'Perfect Storm' and Acute Coronary Syndrome Onset: Do Psychosocial Factors Play a Role?" *Progressive Cardiovascular Disease* (May–Jun 2013), 55(6):601–10. doi: 10.1016/j.pcad.2013.03.003. Epub April 6 2013.
5. For an excellent review of shock and its treatment see: Mines, S. *We are All in Shock: How Overwhelming Experiences Shatter You and What You Can Do About It* (Franklin Lakes, New Jersey: The Career Press, 2003).
6. Zimberoff, D., and D. Hartman. *Overcoming Shock: Healing the Traumatized Mind and Heart* (Far Hills, New Jersey: New Horizon Press, 2014).
7. Bourne, E. *The Anxiety and Phobia Workbook* (Oakland, California: New Harbinger, 1995).
8. Ellis, A., et al. *A Guide to Rational Living (3rd Edition)* (North Hollywood, California: Wilshire Book Co, 1997). Or Ellis, A. *Overcoming Destructive*

Beliefs, Feelings, and Behaviors: New Directions for Rational Emotive Behavior Therapy (Amherst, New York: Prometheus Books, 2001).

9. Beck, A. *Cognitive Therapy and Emotional Disorders* (Meridien Books, 1979). Or, Beck, A. and J. Beck. *Cognitive Behavior Therapy: Basics and Beyond (2nd edition)* (New York: Guilford Press, 2011).
10. For more readings on mindfulness and mindfulness-based cognitive behavioral therapy see: Williams, W., et al. *The Mindful Way Through Depression: Freeing Yourself from Chronic Unhappiness* (New York: Guilford Press, 2007); Orsillo, S., et al. *The Mindful Way Through Anxiety: Break Free from Chronic Worry and Reclaim Your Life* (New York: Guilford Press, 2001); Kabat-Zinn, J. *Mindfulness for Beginners: Reclaiming the Present Moment—And Your Life* (Boulder, Colorado: Sounds True Inc., 2012).

Chapter 11: Seven Essential Tools for a Strong Recovery

1. Anderson, S. *Taming Your Outer Child: A Revolutionary Program to Overcome Self-Defeating Behaviors* (New York: Ballantine Books, 2011).
2. Ford, D. *The Dark Side of the Light Chasers: Reclaiming Your Power, Creativity, Brilliance, and Dreams* (New York: Riverhead Books, 2010).
3. Gallagher, M.W., S.J. Lopez, and S.D. Pressman. "Optimism is Universal: Exploring the Presence and Benefits of Optimism in a Representative Sample of the World." *Journal of Personality* (2013). Epub 12 April 2013.
4. Kato, K., and R. Zweig, et al. "Positive Attitude Towards Life and Emotional Expression as Personality Phenotypes for Centenarians." *Aging* (May 2012), 4(5):359–67
5. Emmons, R., and M. McCullough. "Counting Blessings versus Burdens: An Experimental Investigation of Gratitude and Subjective Well-Being in Daily Life." *Journal of Personality and Social Psychology* (2003), Vol. 84, No. 2, 377–389.
6. Homer, B., and P. Halkitis, et al. "Methamphetamine Use and HIV in Relation to Social Cognition." *Journal of Health Psychology* (2012), 18(7) 900–910.
7. See reference section on empathy.

Epilogue

1. Rofes, E. "Gay Bodies, Gay Selves: Understanding the Gay Men's Health Movement." *White Crane Journal* (Fall 2005).

Appendix: Other Substances Frequently Used with Methamphetamine

1. Curran, H.V., H. Rees, T. Hoare, R. Hoshi, and A. Bond. "Empathy and Aggression: Two Faces of Ecstasy? A Study of Interpretative Cognitive Bias and Mood Change in Ecstasy Users." *Psychopharmacology* (January 2004).

2. Plankey, M.W., D.G. Ostrow, and R. Stall, et al. "The Relationship Between Methamphetamine and Popper Use with HIV Seroconversion in the Multicenter AIDS Cohort Study." *Journal of Acquired Immune Deficiency Syndrome* (2007). Published online, ahead of print March 2007.
3. Mansergh, G. "Crystal Use, Viagra Use, and Specific Sexual Risk Behaviors of Men Who Have Sex with Men (MSM) During a Recent Anal Sex Encounter." Paper presented at the 2004 National STD Prevention Conference (Philadelphia, Pennsylvania: 2004).
4. Mansvelder, H.D., J.R. Keath, and D.S. McGehee. "Synaptic Mechanisms Underlie Nicotine-Induced Excitability of Brain Reward Areas." *Neuron* (2002), 33(6):905–919.

Recommended Reading

Sexual Desire

Bader, Michael. *Arousal: the Secret Logic of Sexual Fantasies*. New York: St. Martin's Press, 2002.

Kinsey, Alfred, W.B. Pomeroy, and C.M. Martin. *Sexual Behavior in the Human Male*. Philadelphia: W.B. Saunders and Co, 1948.

Kinsey, Alfred, W.B. Pomeroy, C.M. Martin, and P. Gebhard. *Sexual Behavior in the Human Female*. Philadelphia: W.B. Saunders and Co, 1953.

Masters, William, and Virginia Johnson. *Human Sexual Response*. New York: Bantam Books, 1966.

Masters, William, and Virginia Johnson. *Human Sexual Inadequacy*. New York: Bantam Books, 1970.

Money, John. *Gay, Straight, and In-Between*. New York: Oxford University Press, 1988.

Money, John. *Lovemaps: Clinical Concepts of Sexual/Erotic Health and Pathology, Paraphilia, and Gender Transposition in Childhood, Adolescence, and Maturity*. New York: Irvington Publishers, 1986.

Morin, Jack. *The Erotic Mind: Unlocking the Inner Sources of Sexual Passion and Fulfillment*. New York: Harper Perennial, 1995.

Simon, William and John Gagnon. *Sexual Conduct: The Social Sources of Human Sexuality*. Chicago: Aldine, 1973.

Stoller, Robert. *Observing the Erotic Imagination*. New Haven, Connecticut: Yale University Press, 1985.

Mindfulness

Horstead, Sharon. *Living the Mindful Way: 85 Everyday Mindfulness Practices for Finding Your Inner Peace.* Calgary, Canada: Mindful Heart Learning Press, 2010.

Kabat-Zinn, John. *Mindfulness for Beginners: Reclaiming the Present Moment—and Your Life*. Boulder, Colorado: Sounds True, Inc., 2012.

Thich Nhat Hahn. *The Miracle of Mindfulness: An Introduction to the Practice of Meditation.* Boston, Massachusetts: Beacon Press, 1975.

Smalley, Susan, and Diana Winston. *Fully Present: The Science, Art, and Practice of Mindfulness.* Boston, Massachusetts: Da Capo Press, 2010.

Self-Compassion/Forgiveness

Neff, Kristin. *Self-Compassion: Stop Beating Yourself Up and Leave Insecurity Behind.* New York: Harper Collins, 2011.

Brown, Brene. *The Gifts of Imperfection: Let Go of Who You Think You are Supposed to be and Embrace Who You Are.* Center City, Minnesota: Hazelden, 2010.

Tipping, Colin. *Radical Self-Forgiveness: The Direct Path of True Self-Acceptance.* Boulder, Colorado: Sounds True, Inc., 2011.

Inner Child

Bradshaw, John. *Homecoming: Reclaiming and Championing Your Inner Child.* New York: Bantam, 1990.

Whitfield, Charles. *Healing the Child Within: Discovery and Recovery for Adult Children of Dysfunctional Families.* Deerfield Beach, Florida: Healthy Communications, 1987.

Chopich, Erika, and Margaret Paul. *Healing your Aloneness: Finding Love and Wholeness Through Your Inner Child.* San Francisco: HarperCollins, 1990.

Anderson, Susan. *Taming Your Outer Child: A Revolutionary Pattern to Overcome Self-Defeating Patterns.* New York: Ballantine Books, 2011.

Shadows

Ford, Deborah. *The Dark Side of the Light Chasers: Reclaiming your Power, Creativity, Brilliance, and Dreams.* New York: Riverhead Books, 2010.

Jung, Carl. *Psychology and Religion: West and East (Jung's Collected Works #11).* Princeton, New Jersey: Princeton University Press, 1969.

Zweig, Connie, and Jeremiah Abrams. *Meeting the Shadow: The Hidden Power of the Dark Side of Human Nature.* New York: Jeremy P. Parcher/Putman, 1991.

Documentary film: Dick, Kirby. *Outrage.* [A documentary film discussing the hypocrisy of purportedly closeted politicians.] 2009.

Documentary film: Ford, Debbie. *The Shadow Effect: Illuminating the True Power of Your True Self.* Distributed by Hay House, 2009.

Optimism

Boynton, Paul. *Begin with Yes: A Short Conversation that will Change Your Life Forever.* Begin With Yes Publishing, a DBA of On-Demand Publishing/ Amazon, 2009.

Seligman, Martin. *Learned Optimism: How to Change Your Mind and Your Life.* New York: Pocket Books/Simon and Schuster, 1990.

Sharot, Tali. *The Science of Optimism: Why We're Hard-Wired for Hope.* TED Books (Kindle edition), 2012.

Gratitude

Emmons, Robert. *Thanks!: How the New Science of Gratitude can Make You Happier.* New York: Houghton Mifflin, 2007.

Hay, Louise, and Jill Kramer. *Gratitude: A Way of Life.* Carlsbad, California: The Hay Foundation, 1996.

Empathy

Hendrix, Harville. *Getting the Love You Want: A Guide for Couples.* New York: Henry Holt and Co., 1988.

Pink, Daniel. *A Whole New Mind: Why Right-Brainers Will Rule the Future.* New York: The Berkley Publishing Group/Penguin, 2006.

Emotional Shock

Zimberoff, Diane, and David Hartman. *Overcoming Shock: Healing the Traumatized Heart and Mind.* Far Hills, New Jersey: New Horizon Press, 2014.

Index